AF326592

PERSIAN ART

Author: Vladimir Lukonin and Anatoli Ivanov

Layout:
Baseline Co. Ltd,
District 3, Ho Chi Minh City
Vietnam

ISBN: 978-1-68325-929-9

Printed in

Vladimir Lukonin and Anatoli Ivanov

PERSIAN ART

Splendors of Iran's artistic and cultural heritage

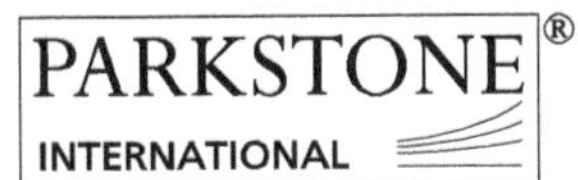

PARKSTONE® INTERNATIONAL

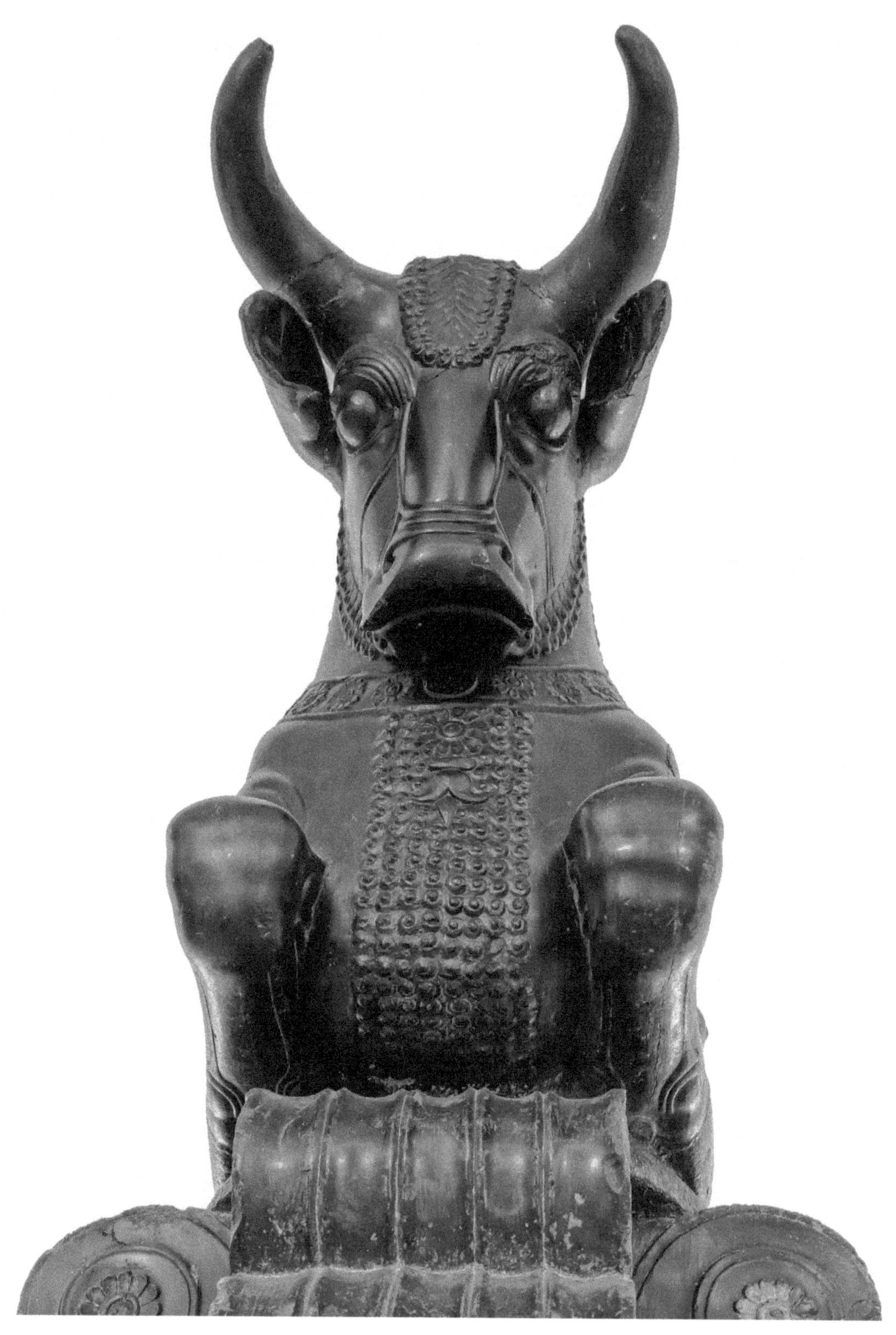

CONTENTS

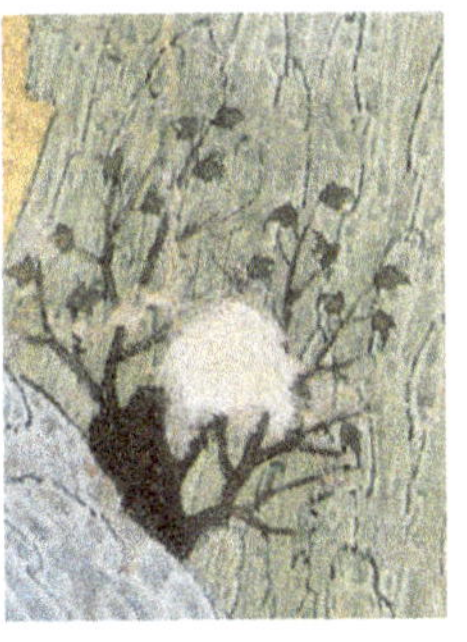

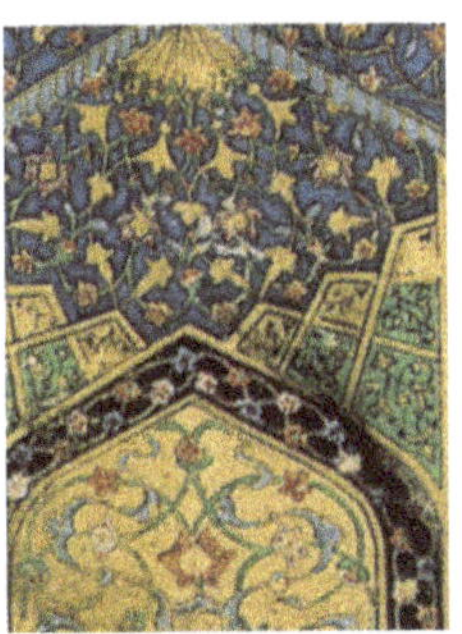

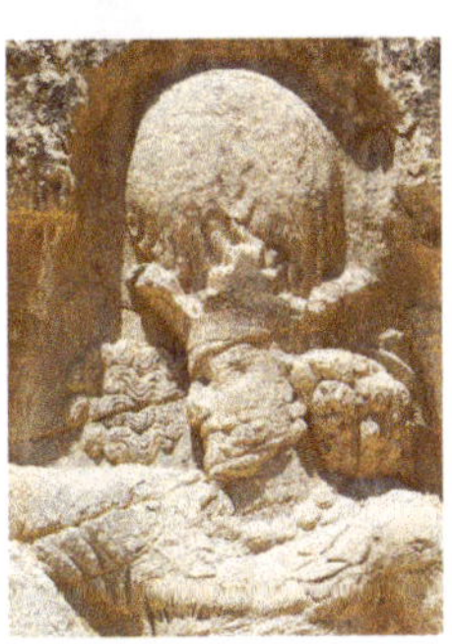

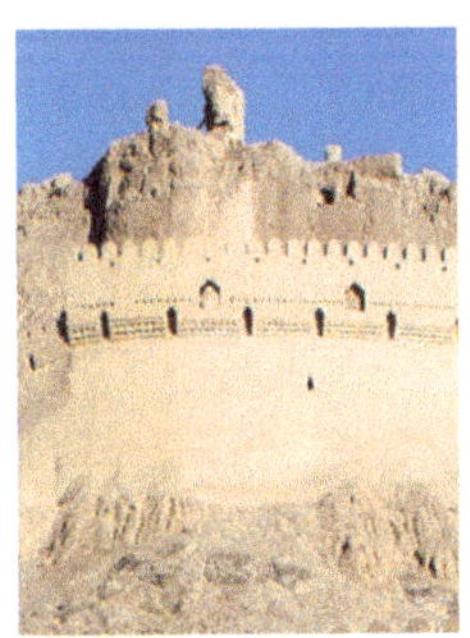

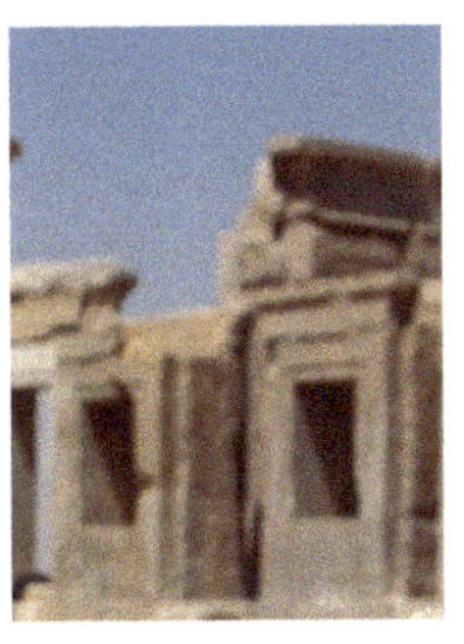

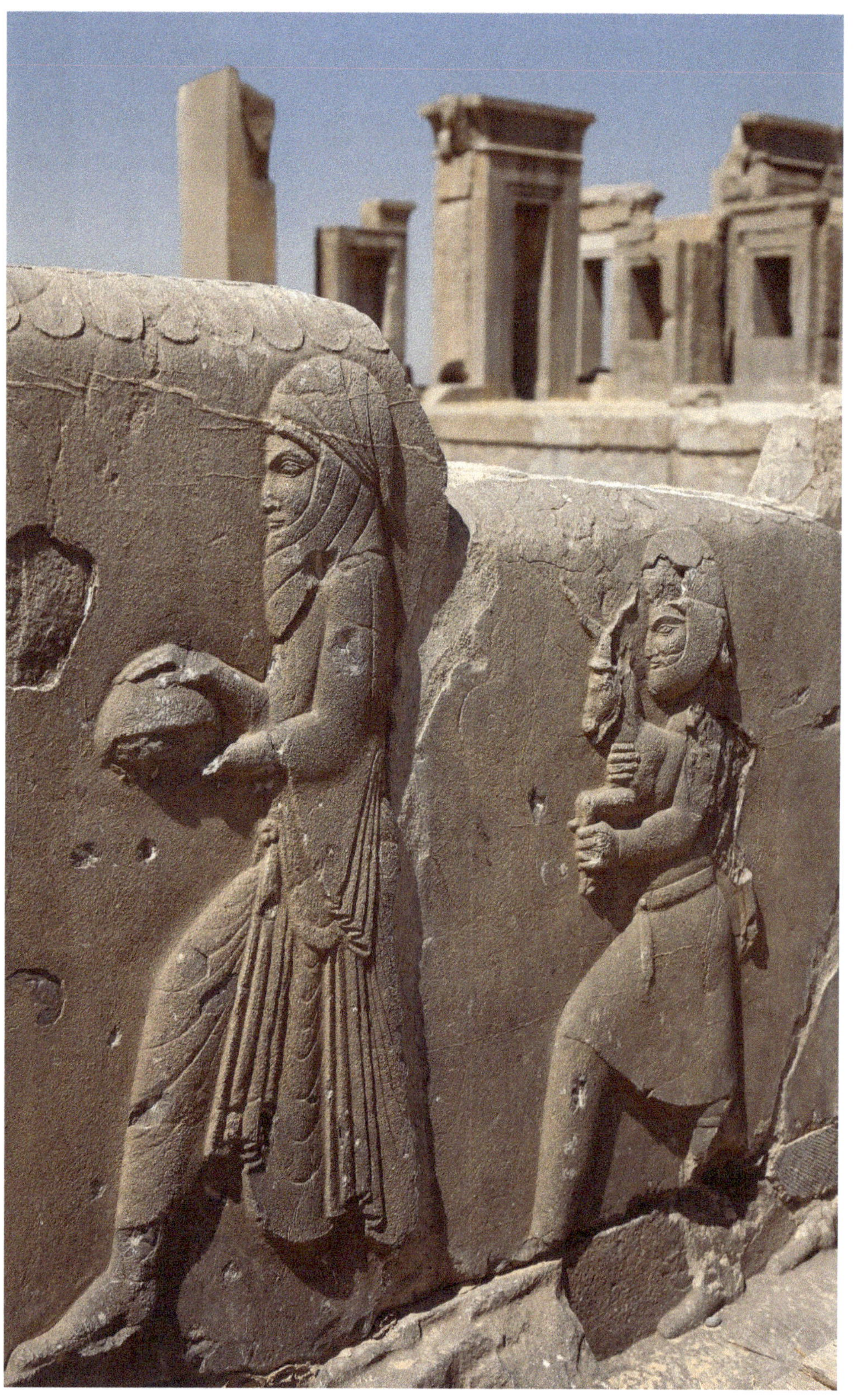

INTRODUCTION

Persian art, though it had periods of ascendancy and of decline, remained coherent, individual and profoundly traditional throughout its development, from its formation in the 10th-7th centuries BCE right up to the 19th century CE. This is despite the violent, often tragic political upheavals, fundamental ideological changes, foreign invasions and their concomitant, devastating effect upon the country's economy.

For over a hundred years, specialist studies have looked at the question of when and by what routes the Iranian peoples, above all the Medes and Persians, first emerged onto the plateau. According to one of the most widely held theories, the settlement of Iranian tribes on the present territory of Iran dates back to about the 11th century BCE, and their migration route passed through the Caucasus. The new ethnic group gradually penetrated into an immensely varied linguistic environment – into regions where dozens of principalities and small city-states existed side-by-side with lands subjugated to the great empires of antiquity – Assyria and Elam. The Iranian tribes, who were cattle breeders and farmers, had settled on lands belonging to Assyria, Elam, Manna and Urartu and subsequently became dependent on the rulers of these states.

It would seem that these questions of the routes by which the Iranians entered the plateau and of how they settled among the heterogeneous native population of what is now Iran during the 12th and 11th centuries BCE have only an indirect bearing on the history of the culture and art of Iran. However, it was these very questions which inspired archeological excavations and research, covering a large area of Iran's Iron Age.

▲ The stone statue of the bull, the capital of the ancient column of Persepolis in the National Archaeological Museum of Iran

◄ Embossed bas relief carvings of servants bringing gifts to the Achaemenian King on the sidewall of stairs in front of Tachara Palace or Palace of Darius in Persepolis of Shiraz

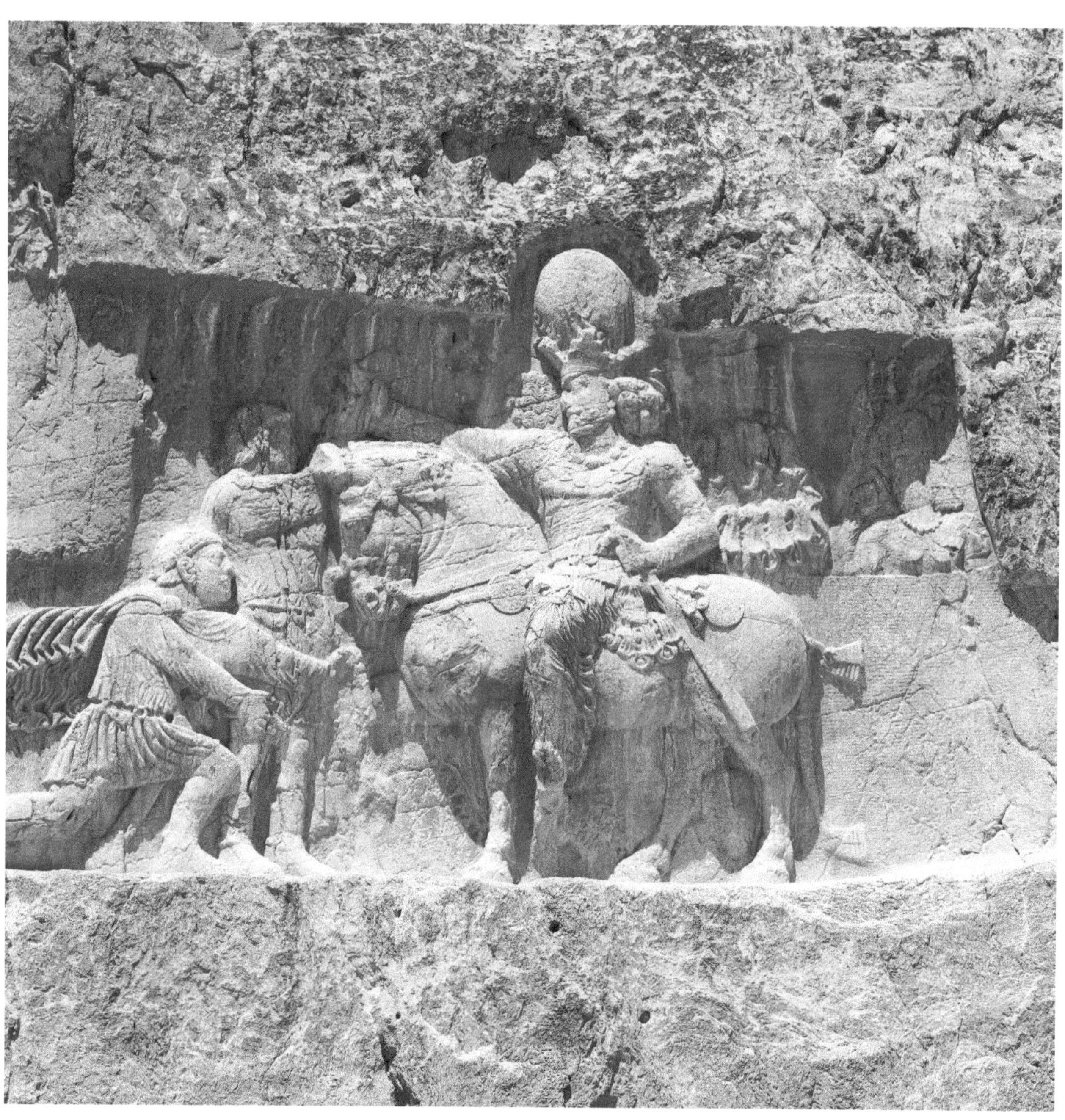

BEFORE HISTORY

The settlement of Roodbar. The archaeologists discovered 53 graves on the hill of Marlik in the form of four different types of "stone box". Golden goblets were found, several of them very large, plus gold and bronze vessels, bronze weapons, parts of horse harnesses, pottery and ornaments. In the summer of 1958, whilst clearing away the remains of a collapsed ceiling from one of the rooms in the fortress of Hasanlu, the archaeologist Robert Dyson came upon a man's hand, the finger bones covered with verdigris from the plates of a warrior's bronze gauntlet and from a solid gold bowl, eight inches in height and eight in diameter.

The fortress of Hasanlu, the headquarters of one of the local rulers, was besieged and sacked, apparently at the end of the 9th century BCE or the very beginning of the 8th century. The gold vessel which the warriors of the palace or temple guard were trying to save was a sacred object. Around the top are scenes of three deities on chariots,

with mules harnessed to two of the chariots and a bull to the other, whilst a priest stands in front of the bull with a vessel in his hand. These probably portray the god of thunder, rain or the sky, the national god wearing a horned crown, and a sun god with a solar disc and wings. In all there are more than twenty different figures on the vessel – gods, heroes, beasts and monsters, scenes of sheep being sacrificed, a hero battling with a dragon man, the ritual slaughter of a child, the flight of a girl on an eagle. In 1962, the Archaeological Service of Iran sent a scientific expedition to Gilvan, about nine miles west of the "stone box". Golden goblets were found, several of them very large, plus gold and bronze vessels, bronze weapons, parts of horse harnesses, pottery and ornaments.

For the first time, we are encountering an example of the formation of Persian art as a whole. On the basis of this example it is already possible to suggest that Persian art was created from heterogeneous quotations taken out of context, from elements of religious imagery from various ancient eastern civilizations reinterpreted and adapted by local artists to illustrate their myths or to depict their deities.

In 1946, an enormous hoard was discovered by chance not far from Hasanlu and Ziwiye. In 1950, the "Ziwiye fashion" began. The activities of antique dealers led to the dispersal of objects from the hoard into private collections, though some ended up in museums in the USA, France, Canada, the United Kingdom, and Japan. Until the 1980s a large part of the treasure was kept in the Tehran Archaeological Museum.

The entire hill had been riddled with holes dug by treasure seekers. Remains of the walls of a small fort which once stood on the hill have been found. Judging by the pottery found there, it was built between the end of the 8th and the middle of the 7th centuries BCE. One of those who studied the hoard remarked: "Unfortunately, what is left in an empty stable after a horse has been stolen merely tells us that a horse was once there, but it does not identify the horse."

Amongst the objects from Ziwiye are many ivory plaques with various designs. Some of them, fashioned with unusual artistry, are undoubtedly Assyrian, similar to those discovered in the Assyrian palaces of Arslan Tash, Nimrud or Kuyunjik. These are all prestigious items. Richly decorated weapons, insignias of a king's or courtier's power, such as a pectoral, a diadem, a gold belt and so on. On nearly all these objects the composition is based on heraldic principles, symmetrical scenes depicting mythical creatures are displayed on either side of the Tree of Life. There are no less than ten versions of the Tree of Life from Ziwiye, consisting of standard S-shaped curves woven into a complex pattern.

The representations of the Tree of Life on Urartian bronze belts of the 13th-7th centuries BCE form the closest parallel. The fabulous creatures depicted at the sides of the Tree of Life on objects from Ziwiye are not very numerous – a dozen in all.

Thus, the craftsmen of Ziwiye created prestigious objects such as symbols of power (ceremonial weapons, a pectoral, a diadem, a belt, etc.), employing the pictorial language of Urartu, Assyria, Elam, Syria, Phoenicia and, lastly, the "animal style" of the Scythians, so that their own pictorial language was again created from elements extracted from various alien contexts to produce a new text. They also employed many older metalwork techniques.

Some of the objects from Ziwiye were produced for Iranian, and in all likelihood Median, rulers. The metalworkers, successors to the Hasanlu and Marlik "school", produced works of art on the same principle as did the Marlik craftsmen, depicting in a single object images of "evil demons" and "good genii" extracted from the context of various religious pictorial systems. In making the selection, no great importance has been attached to the symbolism these images possessed in their own pictorial systems.

It is only in late Zoroastrian works that we find faint hints of anthropomorphic representation. In

Blur in iran persepolis the old ruins historical ▶
destination monuments and ruin

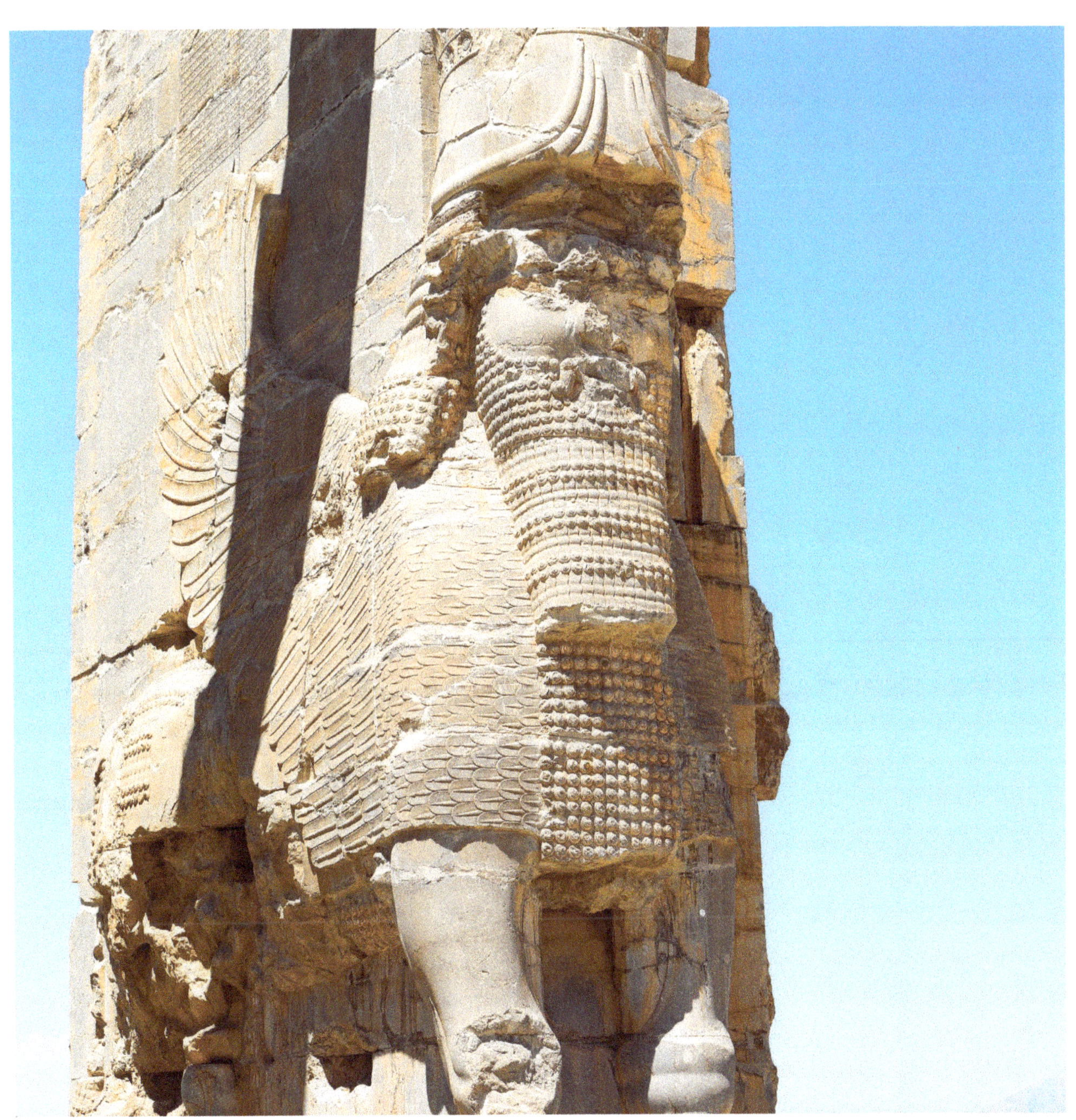

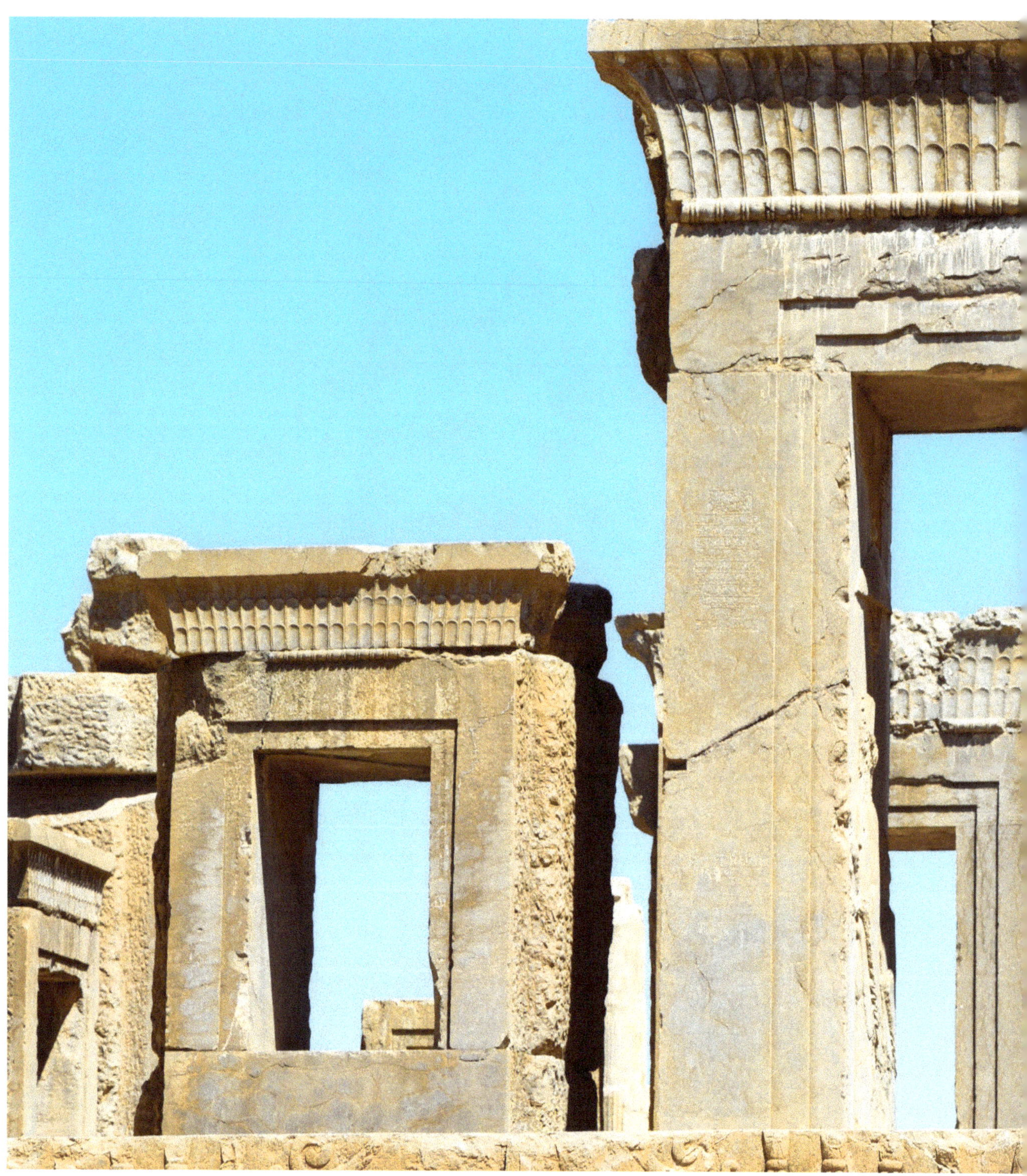

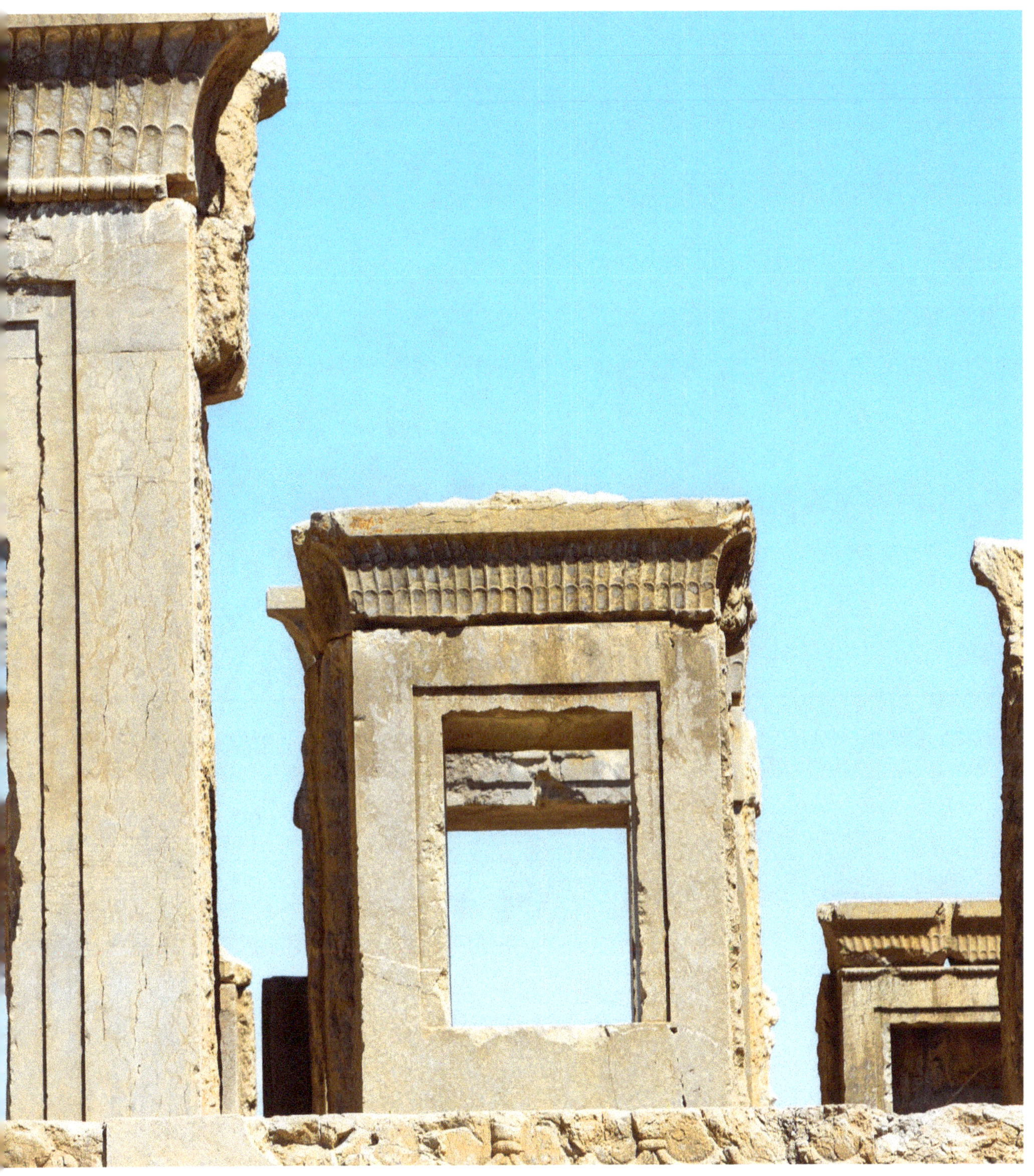

▲ Blur in iran persepolis the old ruins historical destination monuments and ruin

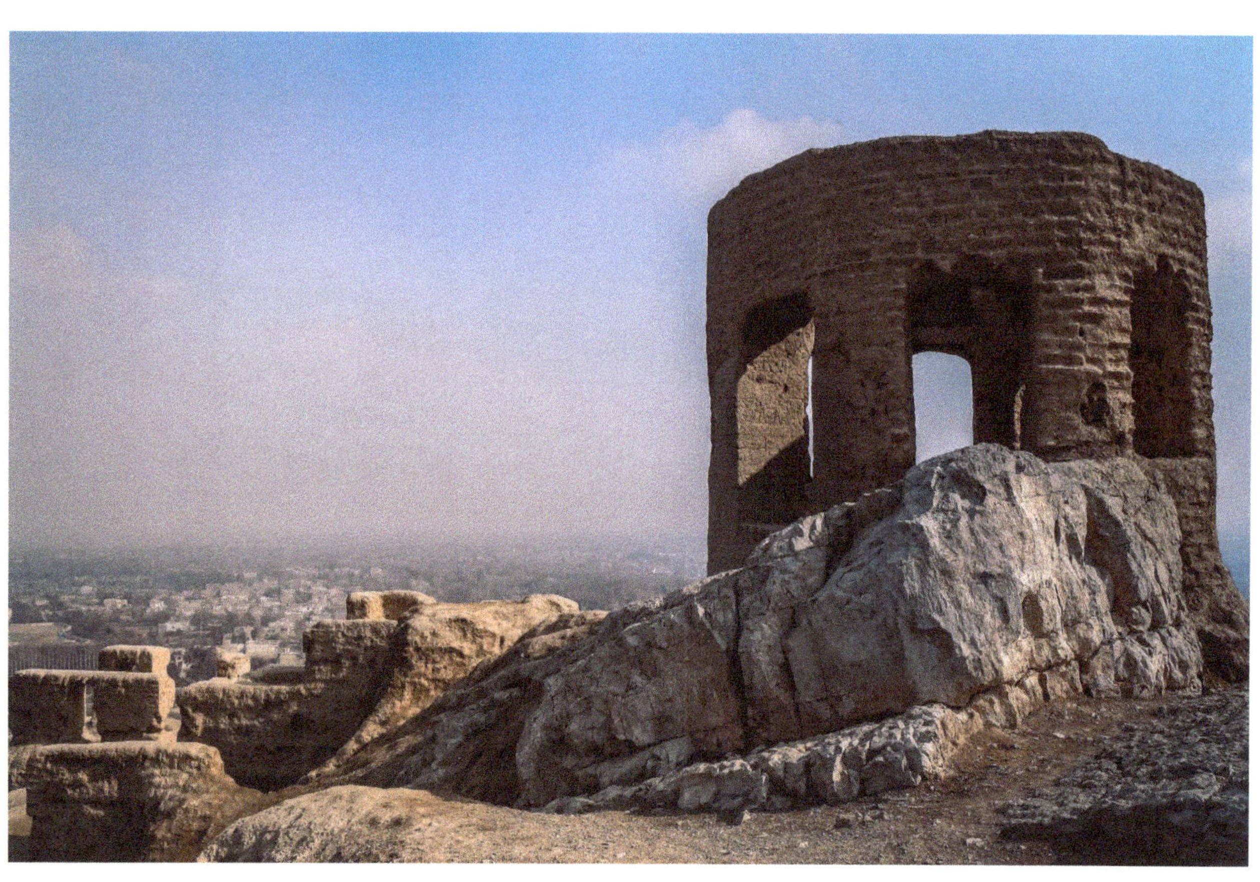

▲ Ruins of the Zoroastrian Fire Temple - Tower of Ateshkadeh-ye , Esfahan, Iran

fact, only a single Iranian goddess – the goddess Anahita – is depicted anthropomorphically. All the other deities of the ancient Iranian religion are represented abstractly, only through their incarnations, chiefly as certain birds or beasts. The Yasna Haptanhaiti – one of the oldest parts of the Avesta, the ancient Iranian sacred text – mentions the worship of mythical creatures such as, for example, the sacred three-legged donkey Khara and a few others.

This probably explains why, when the need arose to depict the Iranian gods, artists had to seek a suitable iconography amongst examples of ancient eastern art. It was entirely natural for the Median kings to use the very rich figurative art of Assyria, Urartu and Elam as their basis, and especially the art of that region in which their state developed historically and culturally. At Marlik and Ziwiye a native Iranian representational language was created on the basis of foreign representational languages; this was, in effect, a native Persian art which, by the Ziwiye stage, one can justifiably term Median.

An inscription by the Achaemenid ruler Darius I (c. 550–486 BCE), concerning the construction of his palace at Susa more than a century after the creation of the Ziwiye complex, states: "The Medes and the Egyptians were skilled in the use of gold, they crafted works of gold". As we find out in the following lines when he comes to list other craftsmen – stonemasons, specialists in glazed tiles, sculptors and builders (Ionians, Lydians, Babylonians and Egyptians) – Darius's information is accurate.

We have already pointed out the characteristics that link the pieces described and the art of Lorestan – one of the most distinctive regions of Iran. Interest in the culture of Lorestan began in the late 1920s. The story has it that in 1928, in the small town of Harsin, a Lur nomad offered a local merchant a strange bronze object – an idol with a human body ringed with fabulous beasts – in exchange for a few cakes.

The story may be without foundation but it is well known that when similar objects appeared in the antique shops of Tehran and subsequently those of London, New York and Paris, the interest in them was so great that thousands of Lorestan bronzes were soon scattered amongst private collections and museums and virtually nothing remained for the expert archaeologist arriving in Lorestan, except for ancient graves pitted with holes and entirely robbed of their treasures.

The craftsmen of Lorestan who, as excavations show, had thousands of years of tradition and extensive experience in the field of metallurgy, manufactured weapons and parts of horse harnesses for various customers, among whom were kings, princes and chiefs of tribes of different ethnic origins.

On turning to an analysis of the art forms developed in the Achaemenid empire, one of the world empires of antiquity, we should describe at least one architectural complex, such as Persepolis.

Persepolis, Parsa in Old Persian, is situated some 30 miles from Shiraz in the south of Iran. Its construction began c. 520 BCE and continued until c. 450 BCE. The city was erected on a high artificial platform reached by a wide stairway with 111 steps made of limestone blocks.

On the platform, there is a unified architectural complex made up of two types of palace – the Tachara (an inhabited palace) and the Apadana (an audience hall). The best known of them is the Apadana of Darius and Xerxes – a square audience hall, its ceiling supported by 72 stone columns. On the left side are three tiers of identical soldiers of Elamite regiments with spears, bows and quivers, Persian guards with spears and shields, and Medes with swords, bows and spears. There are also warriors carrying the king's throne, leading the royal horses and driving the royal chariots. On the right side, the reliefs depict a procession of the nations which formed part of the Achaemenid empire. At the head of each group is a satrap – the governor of a province who was always chosen from one of the leading aristocratic families – in ceremonial Persian dress with a high tiara.

There are the Medes with their famous horses of Nisa, bearing gold vases, goblets and torques, Elamites with tame lionesses and gold daggers, Africans with okapi, Babylonians with bulls, Armenians with horses, vases and rhytons, Arabs with camels, and other peoples.

By the east door of the Apadana of Darius-Xerxes; close to the door Darius I, the king of kings of the Achaemenid state, is represented, seated on his throne, and behind him stands the

heir to the throne, Xerxes. The hands of both of them are raised and stretched out in a gesture of worship towards the symbol of the royal deity, Khwarnah. At the north entrance to the throne room, the king of kings is depicted fighting a monster with the head, body and forelegs of a lion, the neck, wings and hind legs of a bird and the tail of a scorpion.

The laws governing the imagery are meticulously elaborated and carefully observed in such details as weapons, dress, headdresses, masterful depiction of valuable vessels, ornaments and details of horse harness. The "portraits" at Persepolis are extremely stylized but the subjects are distinguished by details of attire – crowns, weapons or bracelets, by their position in the scene depicted or by clearly delineated "ethnographic" features.

Having subjugated Media and Asia Minor and destroyed Babylon, the Achaemenid king of kings, Cyrus II (590-530 BCE), became the ruler of an enormous powerful state. He ordered building to begin at Pasargadae, in view of the new political and religious tasks which confronted him. The buildings of his official residence were to be constructed of stone and decorated with reliefs. Median concepts and techniques were employed, or those used in Assyria and Elam which Cyrus had subjugated. In other instances, ready-made traditional forms were lacking, so there was a certain synthesis of other elements. But as all the palaces were to be constructed of stone and at that time such buildings only existed in Asia Minor it was essential to attract stonemasons

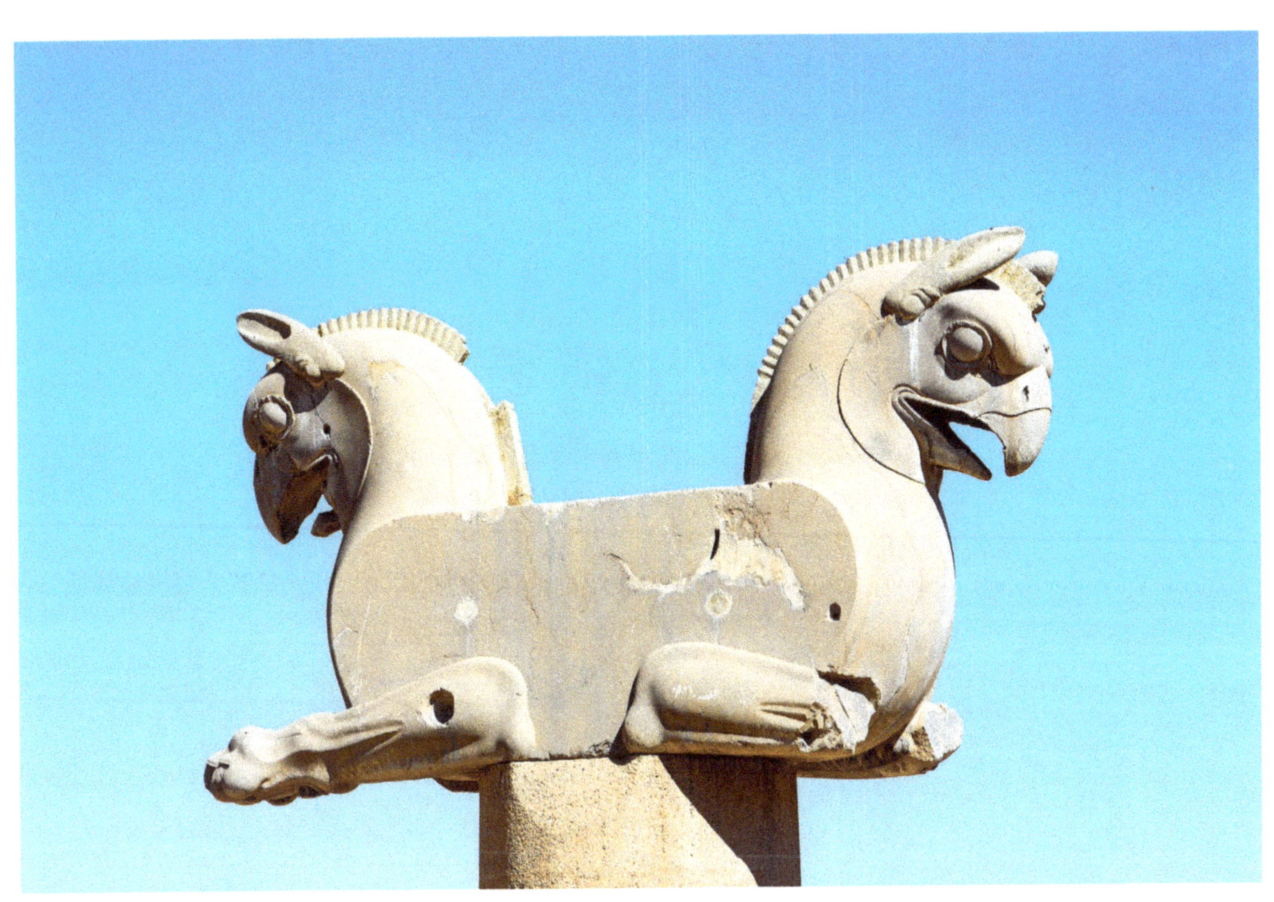

▲ Twin Homa or Huma the Griffin bird figures used as decorative capital statuary of a column in Persepolis of Shiraz

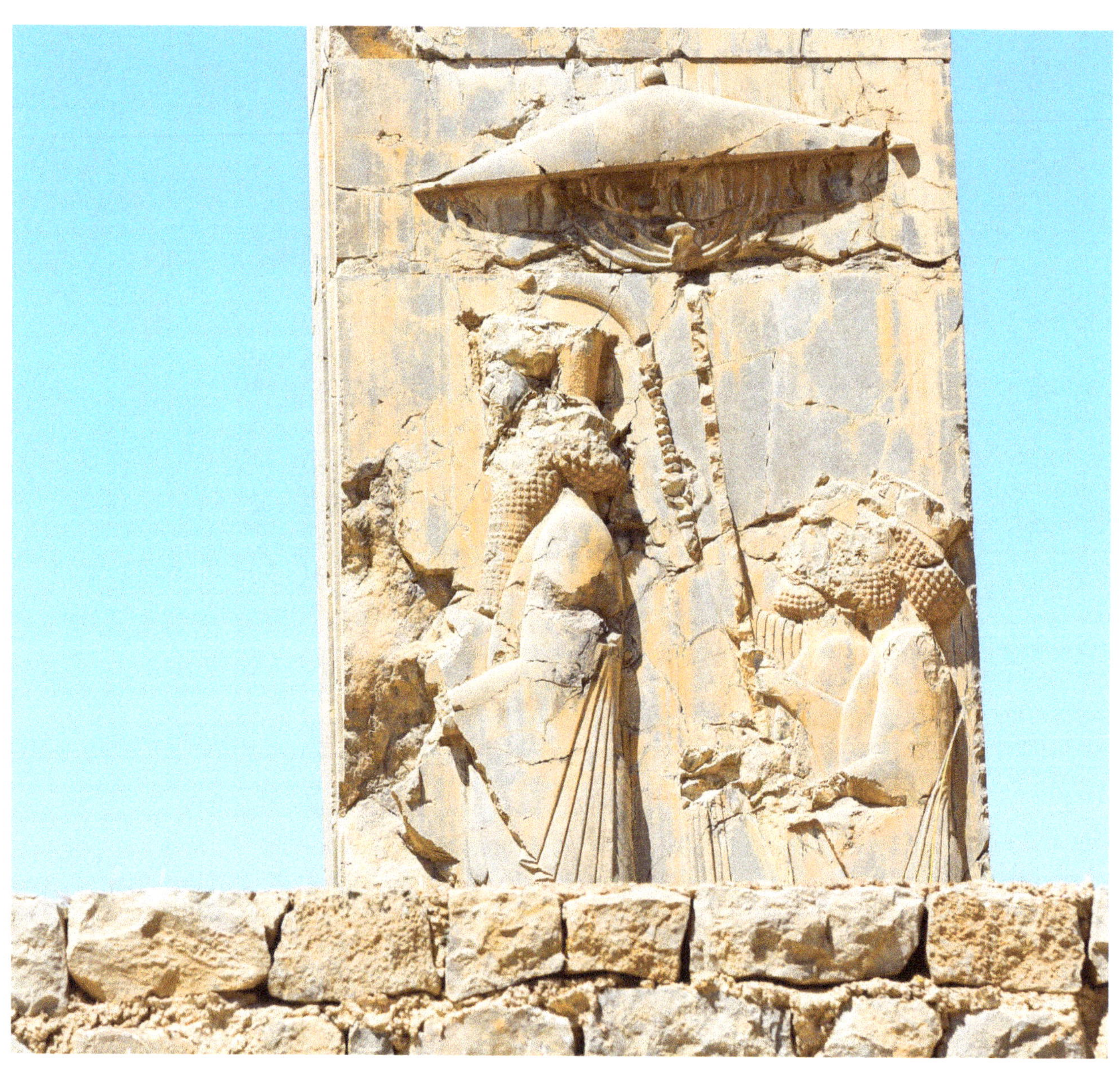

▲ Blur in iran persepolis the old ruins historical destination monuments from Sardis and Ephesus, in addition to those craftsmen schooled in the Mesopotamian and Median traditions who were employed above all as sculptors. A school of craftsmen developed at Pasargadae which later flourished at Persepolis.

The Achaemenid age was the first period of a native Persian art from which many objects have survived, as well as written records. Such of its features may well help reconstruct the history of Median art from a few surviving objects and at present a comparison is possible only of general patterns and theories rather than of actual objects.

The paradox of Achaemenid art lies in the fact that all, or nearly all, the details of any particular image or any particular architectural construction can be traced back to prototypes of previous ages and various lands, but the image itself, nevertheless, remains distinct from anything known and is specifically Achaemenid.

The plan of the Apadana at Persepolis, for example, was repeated by Darius at Susa, and in Armenia an Urartian temple was rebuilt according to the same plan; the same sort of palace was erected for the Achaemenid satrap at Khwarazm. In many instances, however, local traditional materials were used instead of stone.

The art of the Achaemenids as we now see it, primarily in the monuments of Pasargadae, Persepolis, Susa, the Behistun rock reliefs and the rock tombs of the Achaemenid kings at Naqsh-e Rustam, as well as in numerous articles of metalwork and glyptics, is in essence intended to proclaim the majesty of royal power and the majesty of the empire. Only such proclamatory themes interested the Achaemenid monarchs.

There is conscious selection, or a strict pictorial system dictated by specific aims. One might say that the reliefs of Persepolis, for example, are thematically monotonous because Persepolis itself was a ritual city. Apparently, the solemn celebrations of the sacred Iranian New Year (Nawruz) were performed here when the coronation of the king of kings took place. We can thus conclude that it is this ritual that is depicted on the Persepolis reliefs, the sculptural reflection of the myths and images of the ancient Iranians. Yet these very images took over the whole of Achaemenid art. Canons stipulating certain "principal" scenes were laid down at this time: the scene of the king's triumphal reception, the scene reflecting his religious faith and certain symbolic compositions. These canons were to endure in Iran for several centuries.

The symbol of Khwarnah, the deity of fate, success and "royal predestination", probably appeared at the time of Darius and evolved during his reign: the rock at Behistun bears an image in which a sphere with a star crowns the deity's tiara and in his hand, he holds a torque – the insignia of power. At Persepolis, Khwarnah is depicted exactly like the king, Darius. The Assyrian "gatekeepers", shedu, repeated on a gigantic scale in the "Gateway of All the Nations" at Persepolis, perpetuate many details of the prototype used and transformed by the

Iranian sculptors, but here they symbolize an Iranian deity – Gopatshah. This image was also very popular in the applied arts. Above the door of the rock tomb of Darius at Naqsh-e Rustam is a sculptural composition that in effect repeats the throne compositions at Persepolis in which representatives of subjugated nations support the ceremonial dais. Darius himself is shown on a stepped pedestal leaning on a bow with one hand raised towards an altar on which a fire is burning. Above this scene soars the symbol of Khwarnah. This scene soon becomes part of the artistic canon and tombs of later Achaemenid kings repeat it in detail.

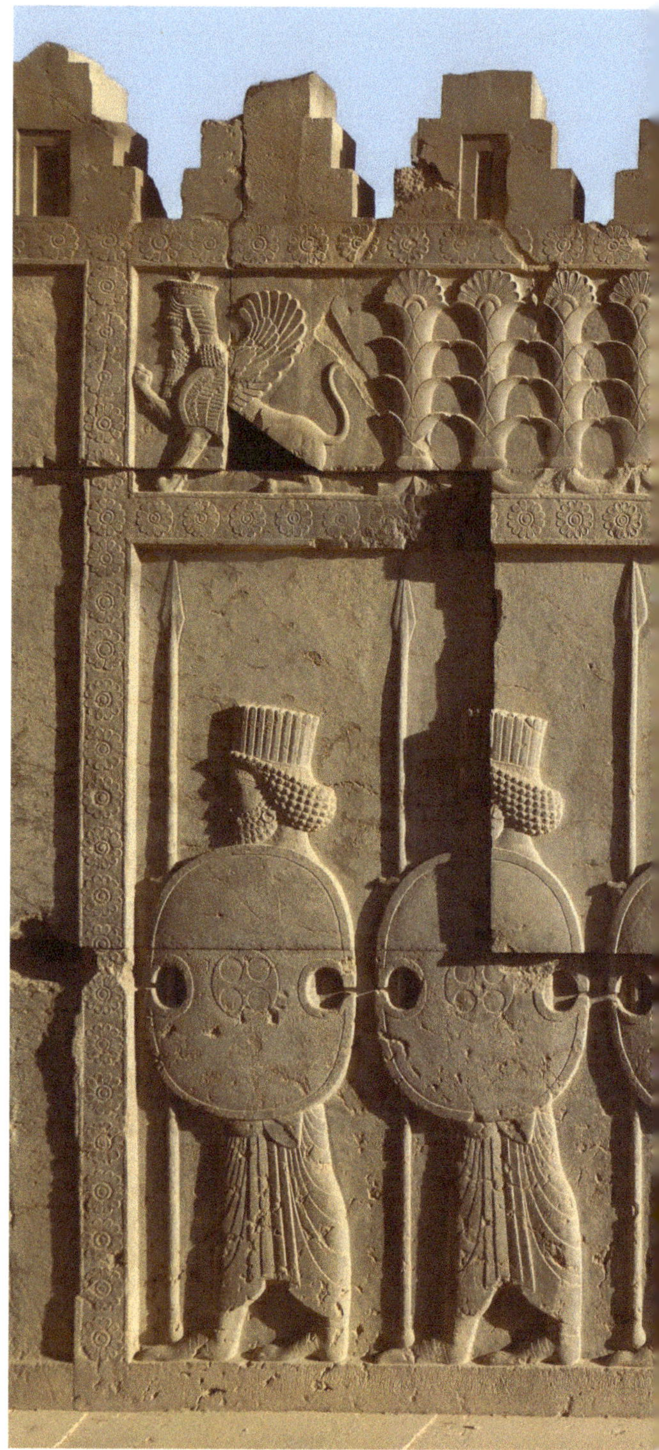

Bas relief carvings of a lion hunting a bull beside ▶
embossed soldiers on one of the staircases in Persepolis
Site near Shiraz belonging to Achaemenid Empire 500 BC

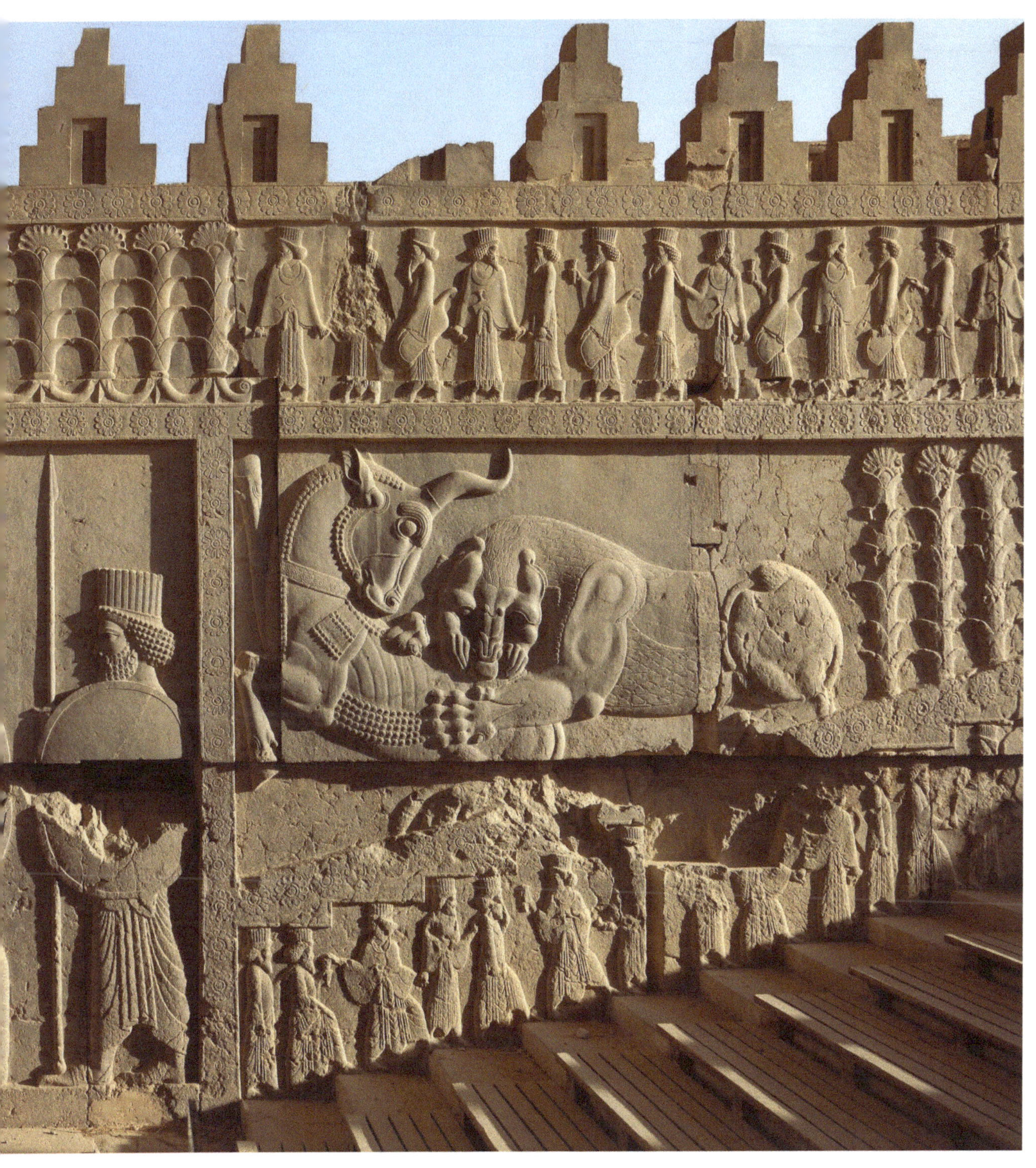

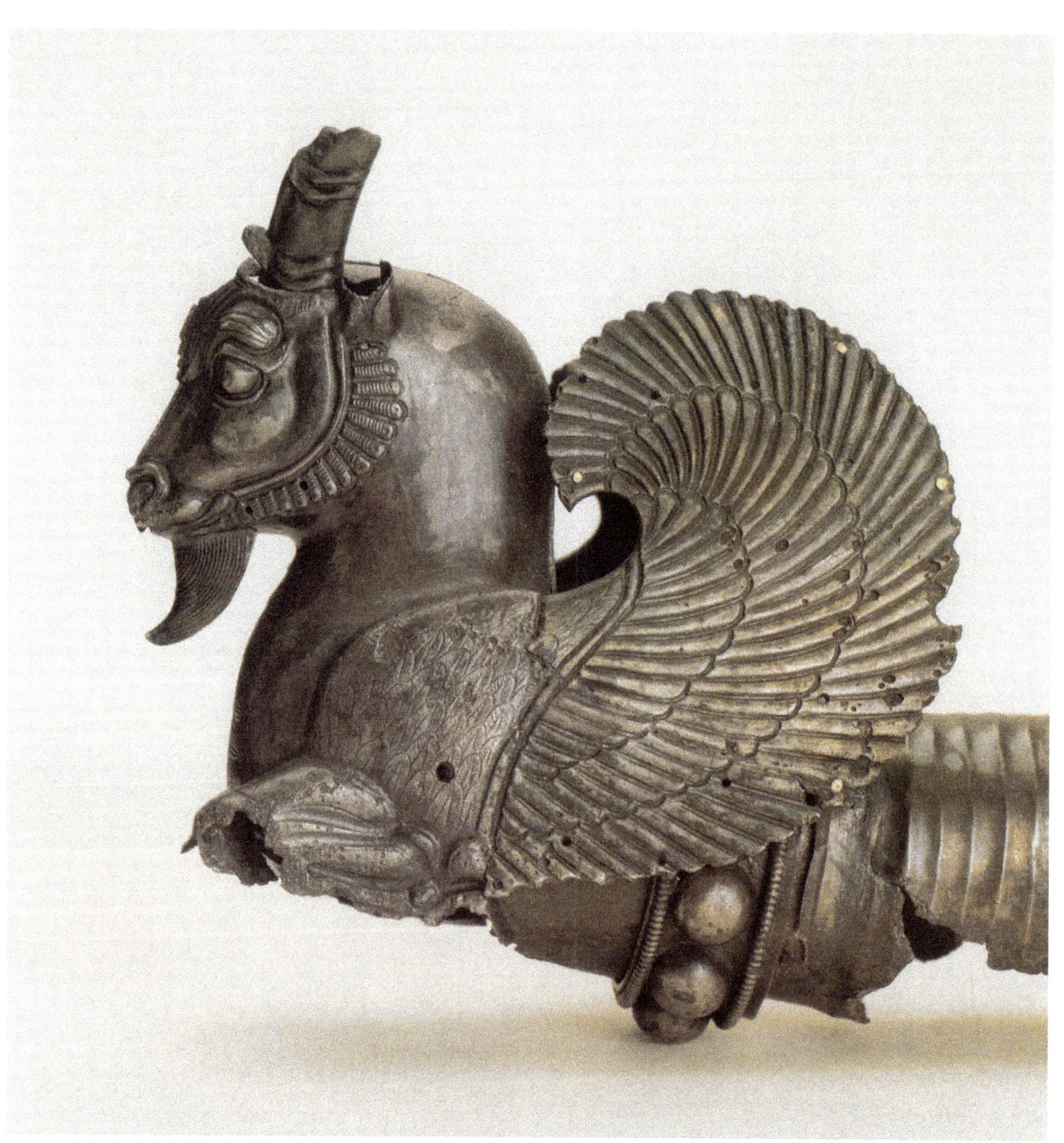

THE AGE OF HELLENISM

n the spring of 330 BCE, Alexander the Great burnt down the Apadana of Persepolis; this event was to be a turning point in the history of Iran and of its culture. Alexander's campaigns in the East began an age usually referred to as the age of Hellenism. Along with Alexander's phalanxes, the artistic tastes of the Greek world, its craftsmen and its works of art all penetrated Iran.

The efforts of Alexander's successors, the Seleucids to create unity throughout lands with varied social conditions, beliefs and customs, complicated by the formation throughout the East of cities granted the right of polis, were simplified by the fact that in theory a social structure and political norms similar to those in Greece had existed in the East even before the arrival of Alexander's troops. As a result, an ideology of "cosmopolitanism" was to dominate for an extremely long period.

◀ Rhyton.
5th century BC
Silver, cast and forged, with traces of gilding.
Length 50cm.
The Hermitage, St Petersburg. Inv. SBr IV. 3.

Initially, the Greeks themselves did not attempt to hellenize the conquered lands. Convinced of the superiority of their own political system and way of life, they nevertheless tolerated local cults and even supported them. In the end there was collaboration between the Persians and Greeks. The Persians began to aid the conquerors both in the creation of the machinery of state and in the sphere of religious cults and all of this simplified the process of syncretization.

Even today the world of Parthian art remains a colorful mosaic of isolated works, varying styles and concepts which it is difficult to amalgamate into a coherent picture. Consequently, it is necessary to bear in mind that Iranian territory during this period is a 'blind spot'. We know a good deal about many works from Central Asia, Afghanistan, north-western India and Mesopotamia, but hardly anything about Iran itself.

In the early Hellenistic period, a common religious language appeared. The cult of a sun deity, under various names – the Semitic gods Bel (in Elam) and Aphlad (in Syria), the Iranian Ahura Mazda and Mithras – spread across the whole Parthian empire. The same happened with the cult of the god of victory

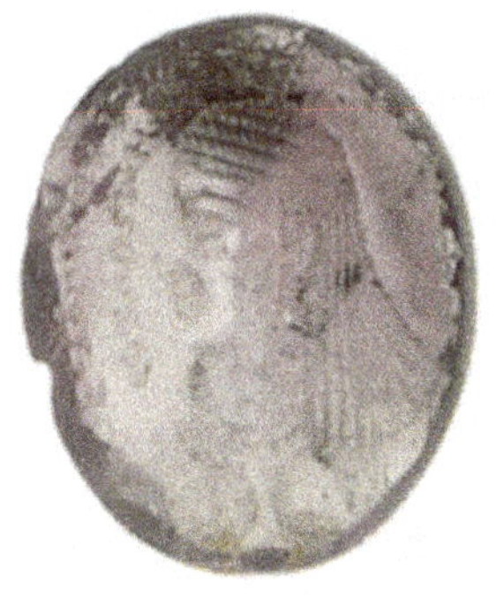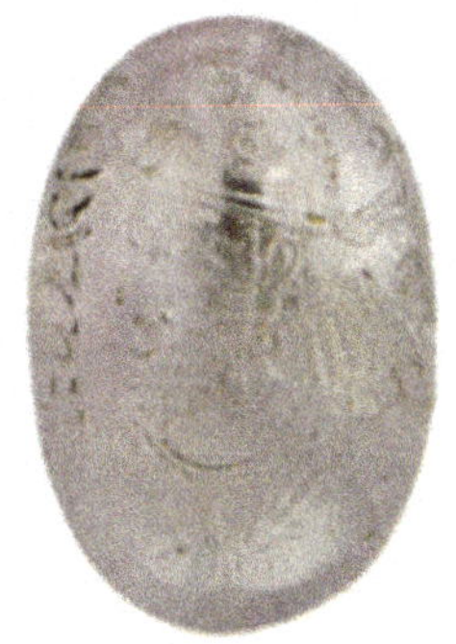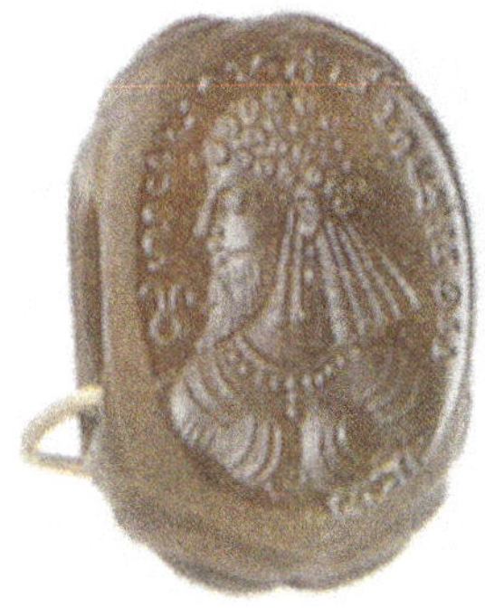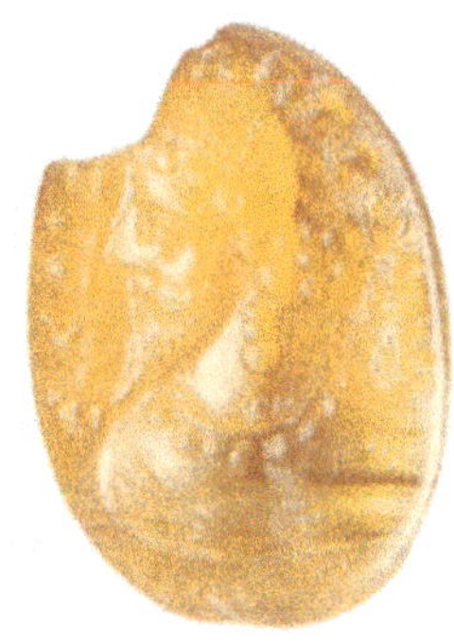

▲ Seal. 3rd century. Carved amethyst. 2.3 x 2.1cm. The Hermitage, St Petersburg. Inv. No. Gl. 979. Acquired in the second half of the 19th century.

▲ Seal. 3rd century. Carved amethyst. 2.7 x 1.9cm. The Hermitage, St Petersburg. Inv. No. Gl. 978.

▲ Seal. 4th century. Carved cornelian. 2.2 x 1.6cm. The Hermitage, St Petersburg. Inv. No. 901.

▲ Seal. 5th century. Carved cornelian. The History Museum, Moscow.

(the Iranian Verethragna and the Greek Heracles) and with the cult of the mother goddess or goddess of fertility, called Anahita by the Iranians, Nanai or Atargatis by the Semites and who was compared to the Greek Artemis or the Cybele of Asia Minor.

During this very period, some Iranian deities were endowed with an anthropomorphic aspect. An enormous role was played at the courts of the Parthian rulers by gosans or minstrels who sang the epic ballads celebrating the exploits of the ancient Iranian heroes, the Kayanids (the kings who first embraced the Iranian faith of Zoroastrianism), or of heroic warriors battling with demons such as Thraetaona, the dragon slayer, or Zarer, the conqueror of nomads.

These traditions were more secular than religious and formed an extremely important part of Parthian dynastic doctrine, for the Parthian kings traced their lineage back to these ancient epic heroes. Dynastic legitimacy was founded on the epic. The epic justified the divine right of the Parthians to the throne of Iran, the epic was Iranian dynastic history up to the 19th century.

Towards the end of the existence of the Parthian state, Christianity arose and spread across its western boundaries. In the state of Kushan, on the eastern borders of Parthia, at approximately the same time, one of the most important Buddhist movements was taking shape – the doctrine of the Mahayana. In Parsa, in the south of Iran, Zoroastrianism was developing into a state religion. Syncretism and the common religious language that had arisen in the Hellenistic period were giving way to the search for a dogmatic religion.

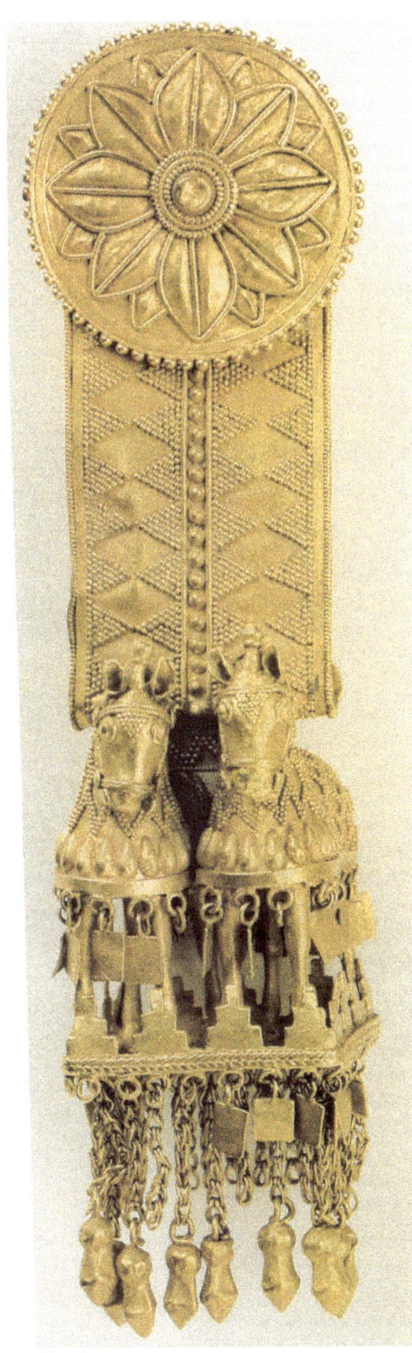
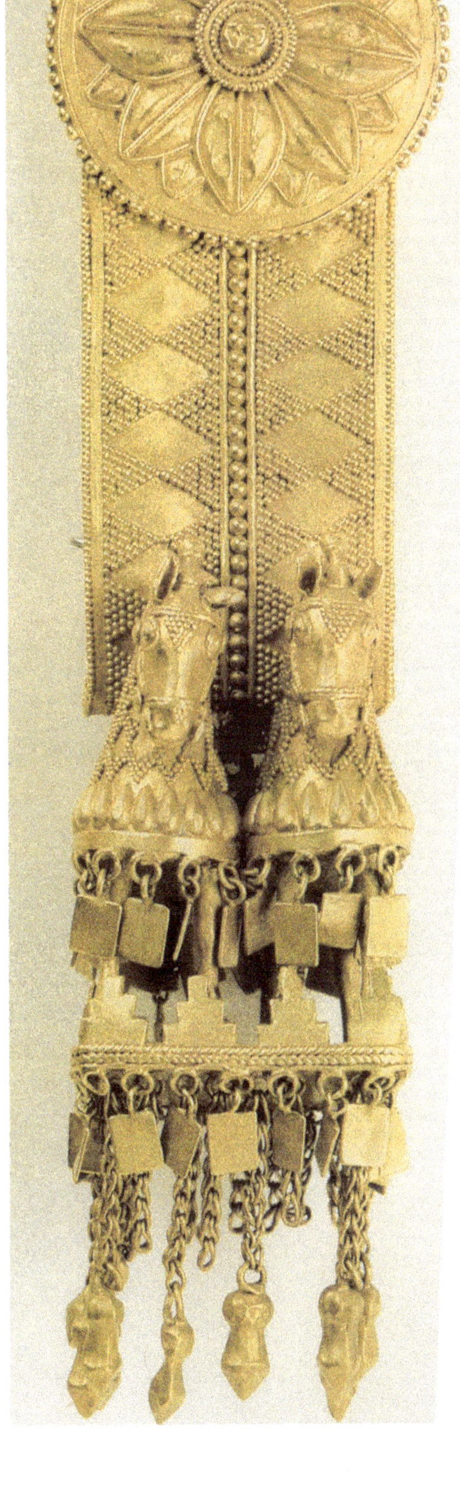

▲ Pendant temple ornaments. 4th century BC
Gold, soldered and decorated with granulation.
Length 12.95cm and 13.15cm; weight 100.73g and
101.07g.
The Janashia Museum of Georgia, Tbilisi. Inv. No.26.
Acquired 1908.

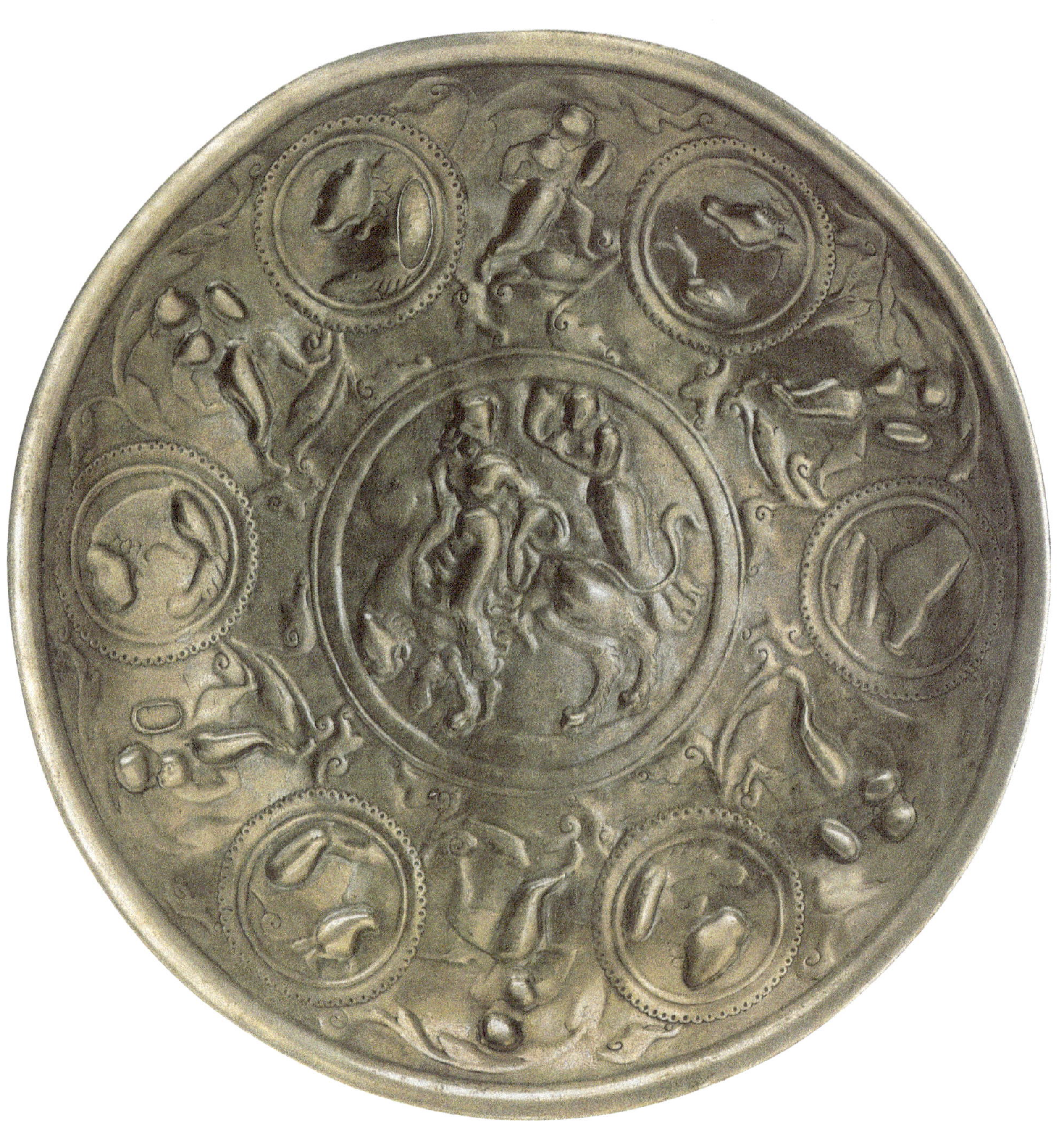

Zoroastrianism

Some knowledge of the Iranian religion, Zoroastrianism, is necessary as it formed the ideological basis of Iran's art for at least two millennia. Its name comes from that of its prophet – Zarathustra. Zarathustra was evidently a real figure, as is corroborated in particular by his "peasant" name meaning "owner of a golden camel"; he was a member of the Spitama tribe and probably lived in the 7th century BCE. He was expelled from his community for having preached doctrines to which its priests objected and went away into the east of Iran, to Bactria or Drangiana, where he was received by a king belonging to the ancient dynasty of the Kayanids, Wishtaspa, who was the first to be converted to his faith. Zoroastrianism is known primarily in its later, Sassanian version. At its heart lies a dualism: this asserts that there are two principles in the world – Good and Evil – and the essence of existence is the struggle between them. At the same time Zoroastrianism is a monotheistic religion, for Ahura Mazda is the one god, a god of goodness and light, whilst his antithesis, "the lord of darkness" Angra Mainyu and his forces, are fiends (daevas).

According to this doctrine, space and time are infinite. Space is dual – "the kingdom of good" and "the kingdom of evil". Within infinite time (zrvan akarana) Ahura Mazda creates a finite, closed period which lasts 12,000 years. The concept of cyclical development is fundamental to Zoroastrian philosophy. Zarathustra's doctrine and his preaching were brought together in the Avesta, the sacred texts.

After its codification in the 5th century, parts of the Avesta were translated into Middle Persian and the Zend, an extensive commentary on it, was written. They contain a number of myths and legends of great antiquity. The gods of the Avesta are not as a rule given human form in the sacred texts. The single exception is the goddess Anahita, who, in one of the Yashts, is described as a beautiful woman dressed in a silver beaver-skin cloak and wearing various ornaments.

Only in one province of Iran, in Parsa, are the old Achaemenid traditions preserved. Here a local dynasty was in power, and although very few works from this province have survived, from about the 2nd century BCE its rulers issued coins bearing their Zoroastrian names, the symbol of the royal Khwarnah and the symbols of Zoroastrianism – an altar with a blazing fire and a Zoroastrian temple.

◄ Bowl with a goddess on a panther and protomes of beasts.
3rd century
Silver, hammered from a sheet and gilded; low relief produced by hollowing the ground, high relief formed of separately tooled applied plaques; chased and punched.
Diameter 23cm; weight 801.9g.
The Hermitage, St Petersburg.
Inv. No. S-74. Acquired 1886.

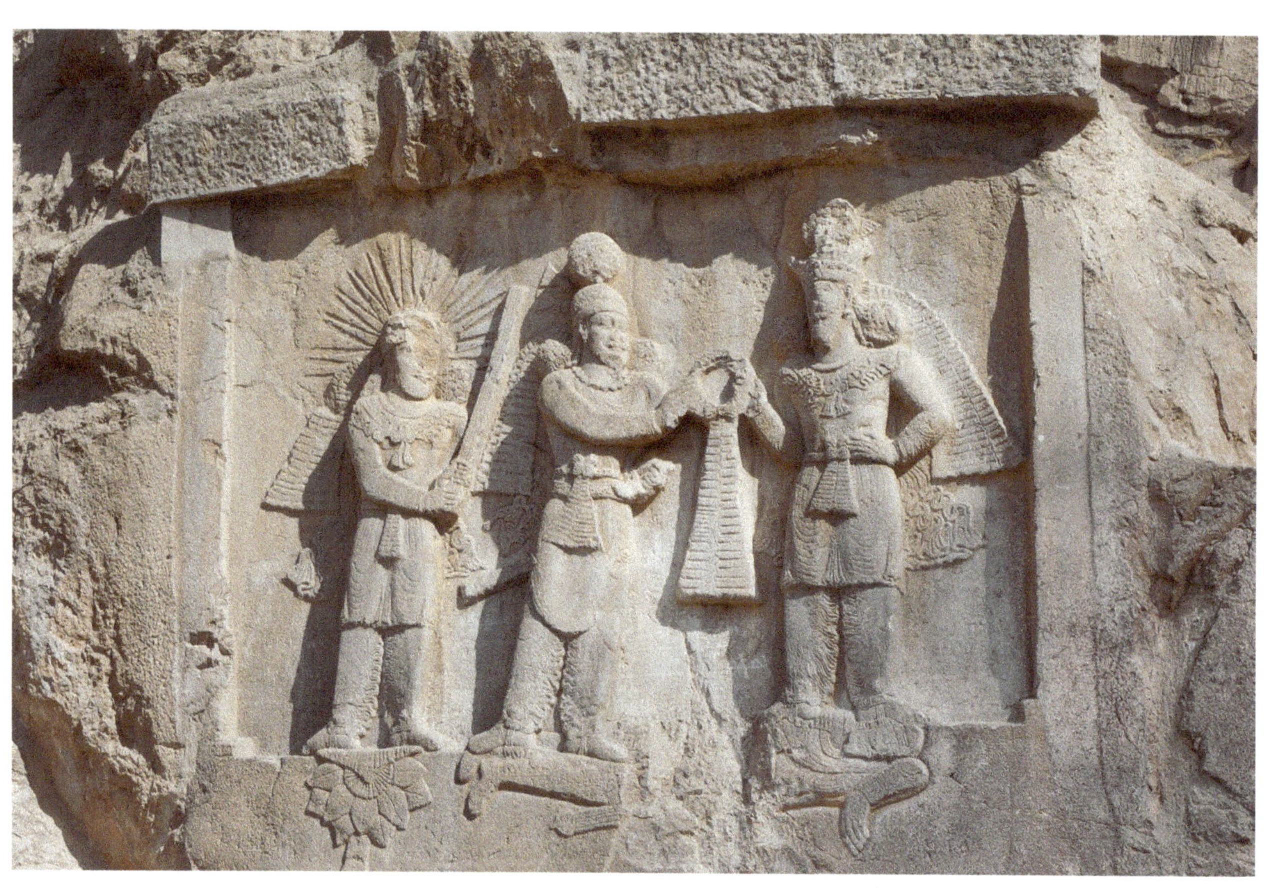

▲ Persian kings on stone relief of the monument Taq-e Bostan in Iran.
Taq-e Bostan is rock relief from 4 century era of Sassanid Empire of Persia

THE SASSANIAN STATE

The Sassanian state, formed in the 3rd century CE, began with the creation of a strong centralized power which fairly soon united the whole of Iran under the control of the Sassanid monarchs.

The keyword in the unification of the country was the "renaissance" of Iran's ancient grandeur and the ancient grandeur of the Iranian religion. Before long, the Sassanid monarchs were starting to trace their lineage back to the Achaemenids. It is natural, therefore, to regard the history and culture of this period as a nationalist Iranian reaction to Hellenism.

Above all, the thematic restrictiveness of Sassanian works of art is striking. Monumental reliefs depict nothing but scenes of the king's investiture by a deity, military triumphs, single combat or the king of kings and his courtiers. In the main, carved gem seals reproduce official portraits of civil servants and priests, whilst metalwork items show scenes of kings and courtiers hunting or again display official portraits. Such was the art of Iran during the course of the 3rd century CE. This period must be regarded as the closing stage in the development of ancient Persian art.

All the basic elements of the individual crowns of the shahanshahs are portrayed absolutely identically whether on colossal rock reliefs and on miniature gem seals, in soft stucco and in silk textiles. Until the end of the Sassanian period each shahanshah was portrayed on such works wearing an individual crown of a pattern that was unique to him and with the symbols of his own guardian deities.

A few palace ruins have survived from the Sassanian period, a few Zoroastrian temples, the so-called chahartaqs – domed constructions with a windowless central space, which became widespread throughout Iran probably in late Sassanian times. The outstanding works of art of this period are the numerous works of applied art, above all metalwork but also carved gem seals, textiles, ceramics and glass, which are to be found in various of the world's museums. These works recreate the image of a state which was one of the great powers of the East from the 3rd-7th centuries CE and a center of learning and culture; a state which not only left as its heritage one of the first medical academies and one of the first universities of the Near East, but also the first authentic chivalrous romance and the first authentic record of the codification of the ancient Iranian encyclopedia – the Avesta.

Religious art also follows the same line as official art. From the very beginning its basic subjects were anthropomorphic portrayals of the major Zoroastrian deities – Ahura Mazda, Mithras and Anahita, depictions of the interior of the monarch's coronation temple and portrayals of the shahanshah's investiture by these main deities. Such works of art reflected the fundamental, divine nature of power cherished by Iran's rulers in a language of clearly understood symbols.

These official works reflected the initial period of development of the Sassanid monarchy's state ideology; they emphasized the real political successes of the first shahanshahs and proclaimed their faith, Zoroastrianism. The religious theme becomes more complex at the end of the 3rd century CE, as if it had become obscured by the introduction into the official portrait iconography of incarnations of Zoroastrian deities of a lower order. The main incarnations of Verethragna are a wild boar, a horse, a bird, a lion and the fabulous Senmurv (half-beast and half-bird).

Zoroastrian symbolism, with various symbols of the guardian deities, occupies an ever-greater place on the crowns of the shahanshahs. The scene of the altar flanked by the figures of the king and a deity on the reverse of Sassanian coins gradually becomes a canonical image. Zoroastrian symbolism, on the other hand, seems to overwhelm various branches of art.

However, the initial meaning of this theme is also lost. The symbols of the Zoroastrian deities – various birds, beasts and plants – become benevolent. Imagery that is foreign to the Sassanians makes its appearance, borrowed from the West and in the main connected with Dionysian beliefs.

In the 6th and 7th centuries CE, art as a whole was characterized by a flowering of the narrative theme and benedictory subjects, although in some works political and religious themes did reappear. There was even an emergence of what might be termed narrative-Zoroastrian themes – various Avestan myths were illustrated in works of art.

The link with ancient Persian art is particularly significant for Sassanian religious iconography. The portrayal of Zoroastrian deities in the form of their hypostases or personifications is a device with which we are already familiar and which was encountered in the art of both the Medes and the Achaemenids. Several such hypostatic images were passed on to Sassanian art. Amongst them one finds the already familiar Gopatshah who has the Assyrian shedu as his prototype, winged and horned lions, winged griffins, the scene of a lion attacking a bull and even such ancient images as a stag, a panther and a vulture. The changes are truly of great significance. The contribution of the late Hellenistic art of Mesopotamia to Sassanian art is also extremely significant.

Vessels of precious metal play an important role in Sassanian art. Such vessels were used at royal feasts, but the feasts themselves also had particular significance. Precious vessels were offered to the kings of neighboring states as valuable gifts; they served as rewards to courtiers for outstanding exploits. They were valued for their marvelous craftsmanship and for their imagery, but the metal of which they were made was itself of no small

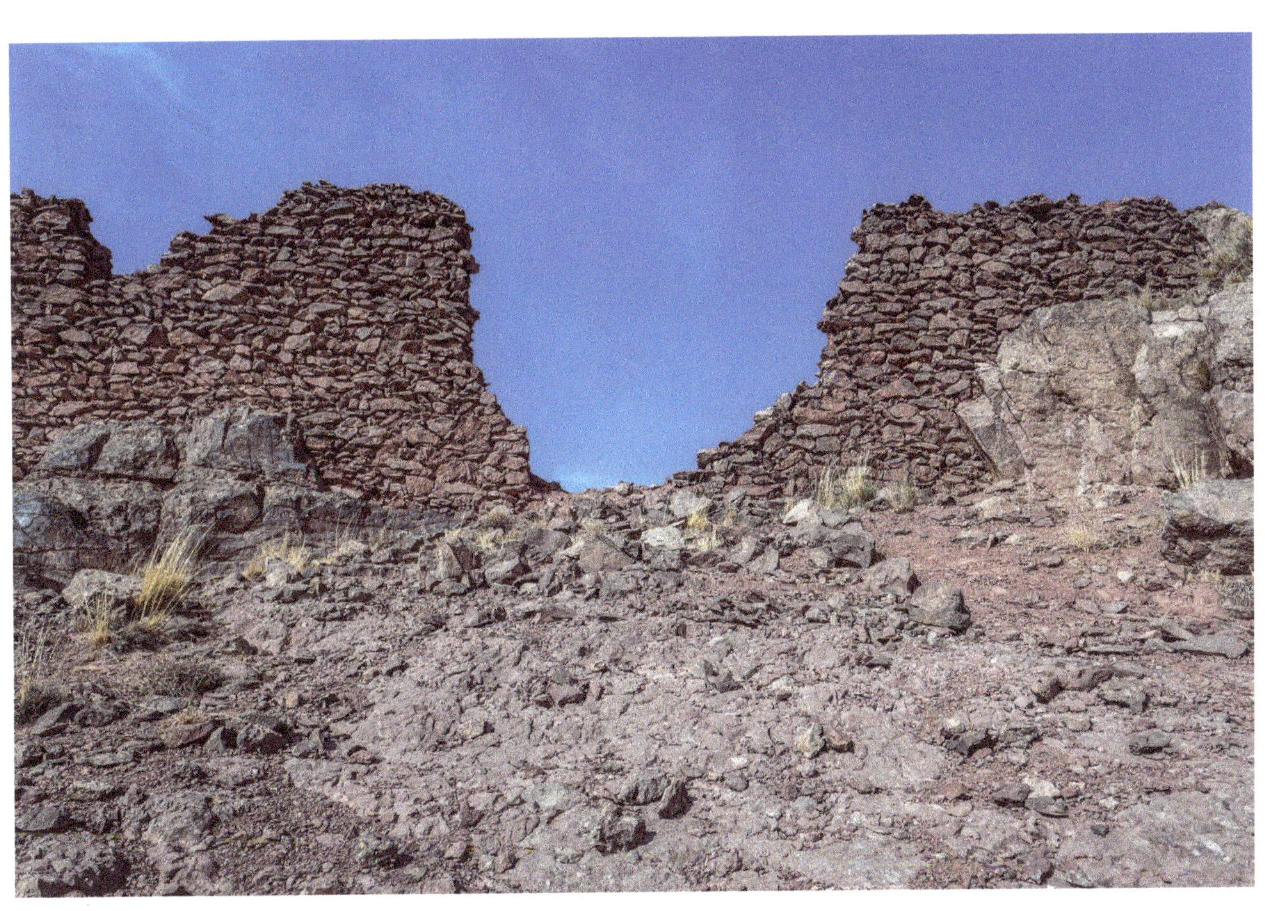

▲ Sasanid era ruins on hills above Abyaneh - one of the oldest villages in Iran

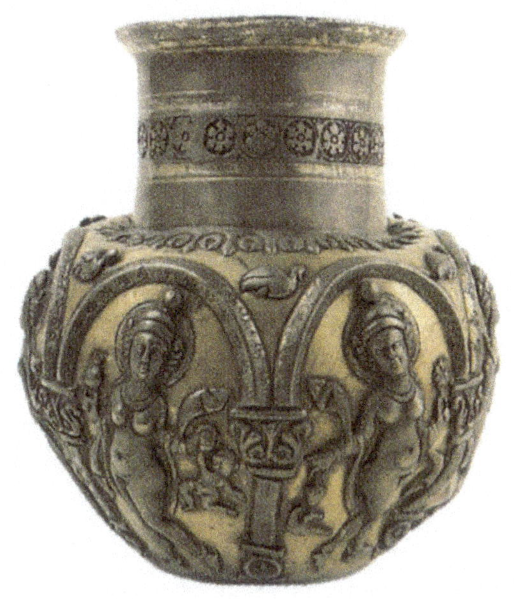

◀ Jug with the face of a goddess.
6th–7th century
Silver, moulded from a sheet, embossed, chased, punched and gilded (the neck produced separately, the join masked by a tooled relief rim). To judge from surviving traces of solder, the jug had a handle. Height 14.5cm; weight 358.3g.
The Hermitage, St Petersburg.
Inv. No. S-60. Transferred 1926 from the Moscow Kremlin Armoury.

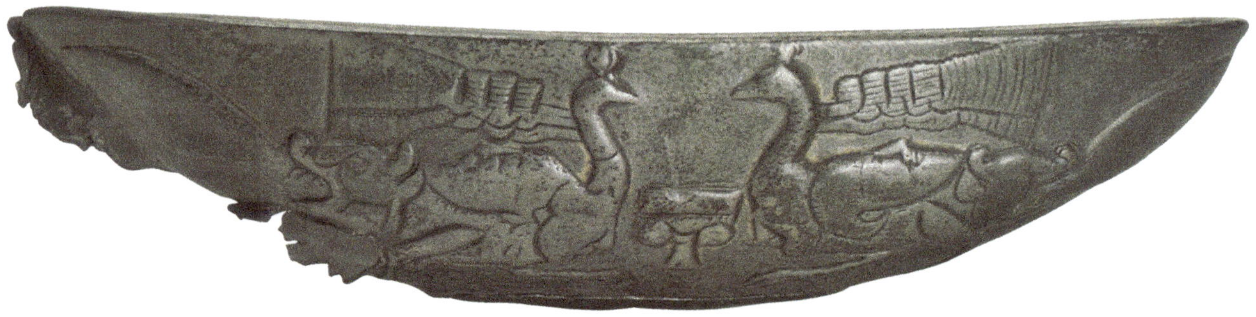

▲ Boat-shaped bowl.
6th–7th century
Silver, hammered from a sheet, with applied high relief plaques. Underneath traces of solder of an oval base.
Length 26cm; width 9.2cm; height 6cm.
The History Museum, Moscow. Inv. No. 83746. Acquired 1947.

value in Sassanian times. The earliest of the silver ceremonial bowls which have come down to us date from c. 270-290 CE.

The first known plate depicting a hunting scene was produced at c. 270-290. This form of art was new to the Sassanians and exhibits some innovations. By the end of the 4th century, scenes of royal hunts on silver plates were gradually giving way to depictions of the heroic or epic victory of the king of kings. This development of iconography is characteristic of the evolution of all Sassanian art; it is a movement from orthodoxy to the everyday subject requiring no religious interpretation.

These depictions are the first and possibly the only clear examples of genuine illustrations of oral or written tales of the skill and valor of an Iranian knight. We find tales of skill and prowess in chivalrous sports and also of proficiency in games. One of those works, Khusrau, Son of Kavadh, and His Page, tells the story of the beautiful women who played the chang and who accompanied kings on their hunts; they are often depicted, for example in hunting scenes of the Shahanshah Khusrau II. A host of such beauties with harps, flutes and changs are depicted on silver vessels – ewers, flasks, deep hemispherical bowls and shallow dishes.

Judging from accounts in written sources, the climax of all the festivals was a ceremonial banquet, which took place after a special service in the fire temple, and various rites in which silver vessels were used. The depictions on ceremonial vessels may be linked to rituals whose details remain unknown to us. These festivities and the carnival

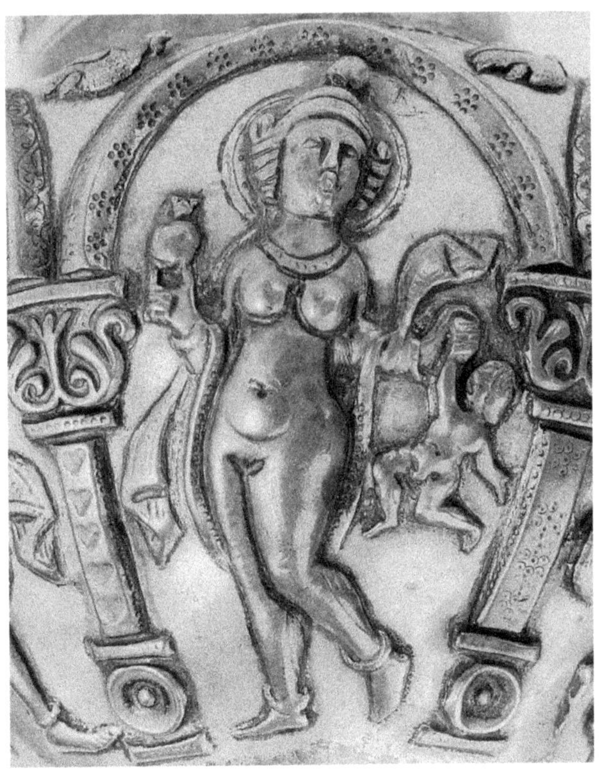

▲ Jug with dancing women.
6th century
Silver, moulded from a sheet and gilded (the neck is soldered); chased and punched.
Height 16cm, weight 871.3g.
The Hermitage, St Petersburg.
Inv. No. S-256. Purchased 1931 in Sverdlovsk.

processions had a definite religious symbolism and ritual significance, but evidently, they were taken over by ancient folk customs and their symbolism. The longer this continued the farther religion receded into the background. Thus, the Muslims of 9th-century Baghdad wholeheartedly celebrated several Zoroastrian festivities, and as late as the 10th century the Muslim rulers of Iran delighted in celebrating the Zoroastrian feast of Sadeh which, moreover, coincided with Christmas.

All this variety becomes confused towards the end of the Sassanian period, its previous exactness and rigor of selection seeming to break down. Judging by those Sassanian items known to us today, it is possible to state that all art of this period, and not just metalwork, follows this line of development, a process by which themes of a propagandist nature die out, and heroic and epic, benedictory and everyday themes come to dominate. This is one of the fundamental reasons why a wide range of similar compositions subsequently pass into Islamic, Umayyad and early Abbasid art.

The Zoroastrian girl mentioned by many Persian and Arab poets of the Middle Ages is of particular interest. She would usually be serving them wine, which was forbidden by Islam, in taverns or among the ruins of a temple. Are these not fragmentary survivals of rituals connected with wine from Zoroastrian feasts, and is this not the reason why there are so many girls with wine and vines and other attributes of the "Dionysian background" both on these Sassanian silver vessels and on early Islamic ceramics?

Thus, looking at Sassanian art as a whole, one reaches the conclusion that it began with a fairly limited range of themes strictly stratified according to genre, as an art that was, so to speak, "conceptual", or at any rate subject to an absolutely specific interpretation, and "imperial", an instrument for political and religious propaganda.

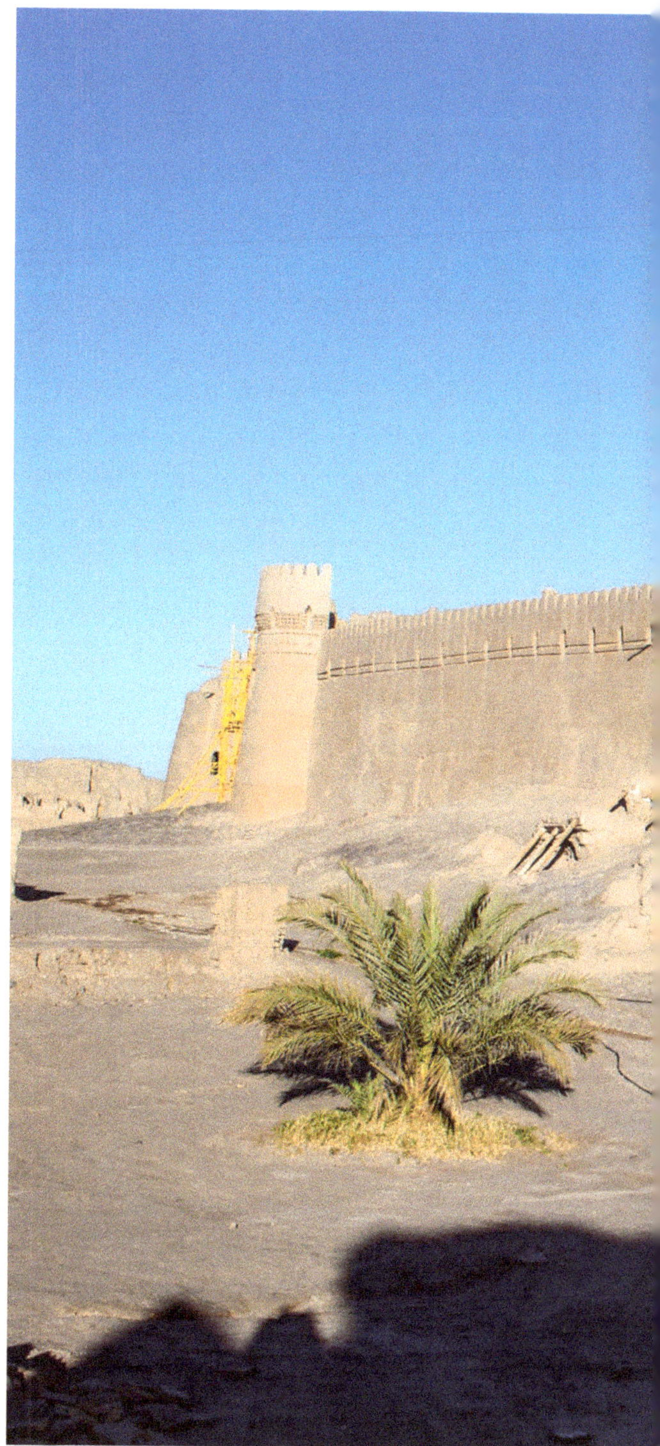

The ancient citadel of Arg-é Bam has a history , to the ▶
Parthian Empire (248 BC–224 AD), but most buildings
were built during the Safavid dynastye

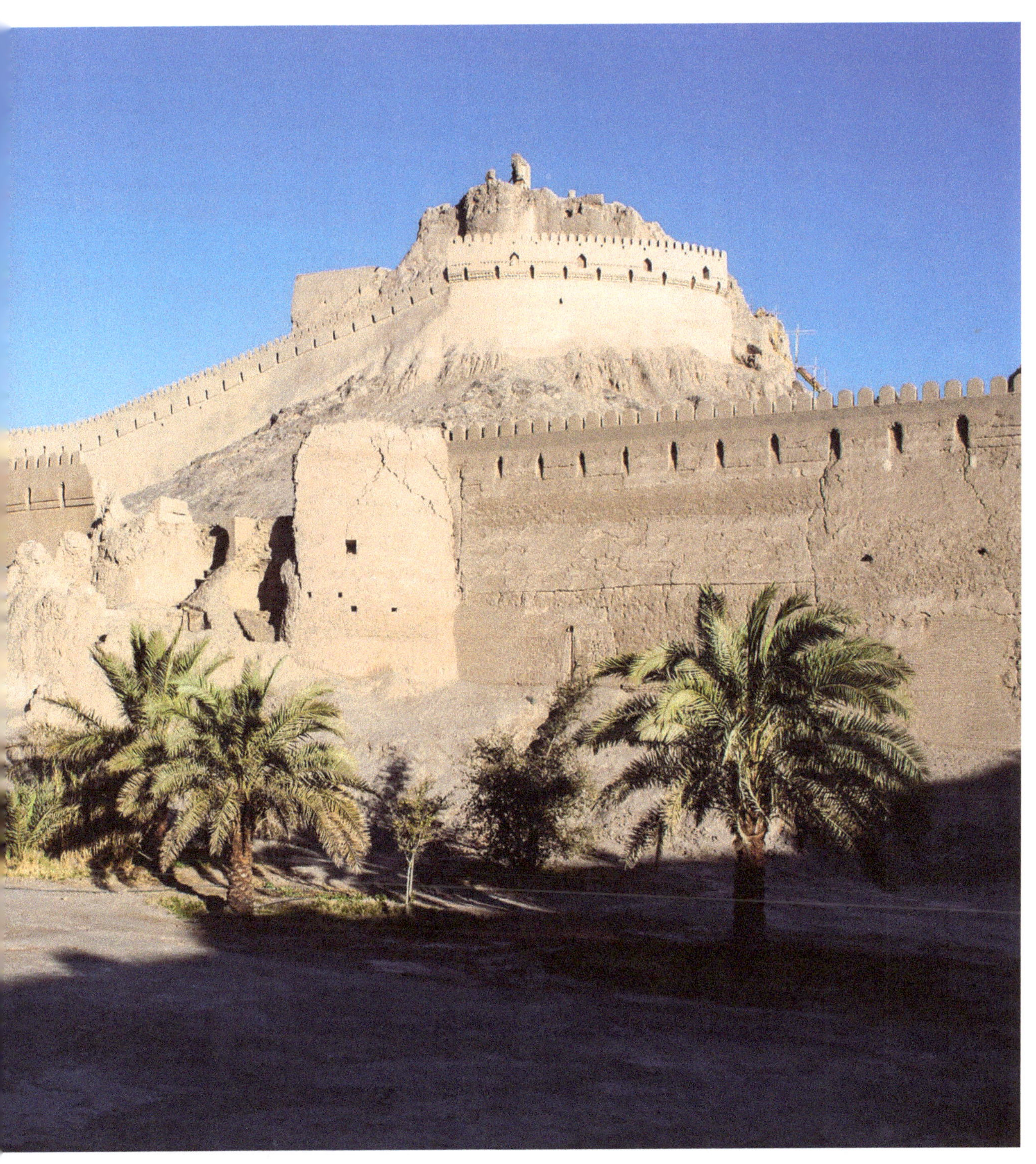

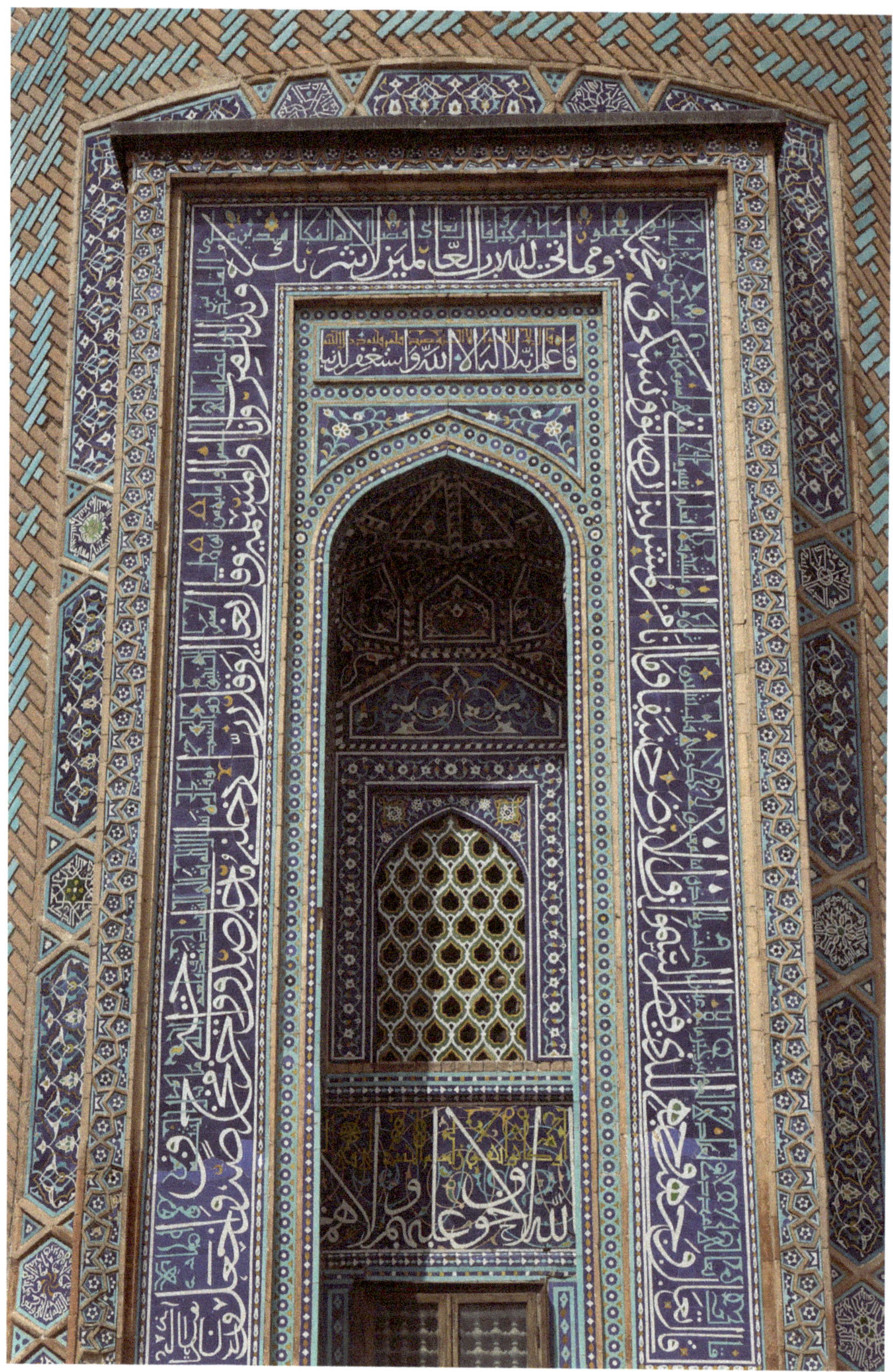

ISLAM AND MEDIEVAL PERSIA

t is beyond the scope of this study even to draw up a brief list of the problems connected with the new Islamic religion, which has been the dominant ideology in Iran from the 7th century to the present day. However, one of its aspects is of great importance. From the very beginning, Islam rejected figurative representation. In this respect Islam differed from Buddhism, Christianity and Zoroastrianism, which made widespread use of figurative representation and had for a long time anthropomorphized their deities. This hostile attitude towards the depiction of living creatures – though in essence only towards anthropomorphic representation as an object of worship – had a number of consequences that were decisive for the development of art in Iran.

Firstly, it caused a gradual decline of monumental art forms such as rock reliefs, stucco panels and wall painting. Secondly, it diminished the status of the artist, at any rate during the first centuries of Islam when it expelled him from the ranks

◀ The 14th century Allah Allah tower of the Safavid Sheikh Safi mausoleum in Ardabil, Iran

of those creating works pleasing to God, and transformed his occupation into something not entirely commendable from the point of view of religious morality.

Thirdly, it narrowed the range of new themes that could emerge, above all the religious ones which were central to all Christian and Buddhist art – the depiction of God and his deeds, the stories of prophets and saints – everything on which an artistic impression of the world was founded in non-Muslim cultures during the Middle Ages.

The Mutazilites (from the Arabic for "separatists") resolutely opposed the concept of God in human form and of his attributes or qualities which were invented by man, even those such as "omnipotent" or "all-seeing", for these are "conceivable" categories. According to the doctrine of the Mutazilites, God is a unity that is pure, indefinable in human terms and unknowable.

The existence of persistent disagreements even between the faqihs (the authoritative theologians) did not, and never could, give rise to any official and general prohibition. Of

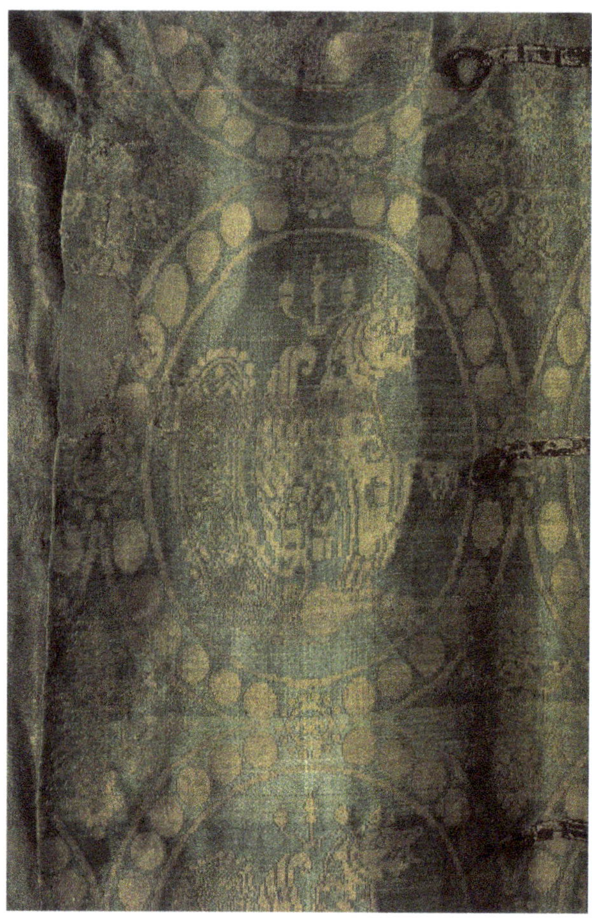

▲ Caftan with Senmurvs.
9th century.
Silk (samite weave). Length 140cm; width 227cm.
The Hermitage, St Petersburg.
Inv. No. Kz 6584. Found in a ruined grave at Moshchevaya Balka (Northern Caucasus).

Ewer. By Nasir. ▶
11th–early 12th century.
Bronze (brass), cast, forged, engraved and inlaid with copper.
Height 37,5cm.
The Hermitage, St Petersburg. Inv. No. SA-12680.
Transferred 1930 from the former Asiatic Museum of the
USSR Academy of Sciences.

course, in the history of Muslim theologians' attitudes towards figurative art there have been periods when a more rigorous attitude prevailed, and even periods of persecution and extreme reaction, but one thing is clear: the question was always one of religious anthropomorphism – and of that alone.

Therefore, there is absolutely no reason to see figurative art in Islamic culture as the perpetual overcoming of a prohibition existing within the religion. On the other hand, the arrival of Islam in Iran brought about the abolition of other restrictions which had an important bearing on the development of art.

By the 8th century the Islamic state, the Caliphate, included not only the whole territory of Iran but also part of Byzantium, North Africa, the Iberian Peninsula, Central Asia and Afghanistan, and it subsequently extended even further; yet this state was by no means a world empire like the empires of the Achaemenids or the Sassanids. Its ruler, the caliph, inherited from the prophet the Imamate, the spiritual leadership of the Muslim community, and the Emirate political power. According to Islamic law, he either had to be elected by the whole community, or appoint a successor during his lifetime, with the approval of the faqihs. And although it was considered that the power of the caliphs had been established by God, the Islamic state was theocratic but far from despotic.

In theory, the Islamic state was considered to be a state of equals and the basic confrontation

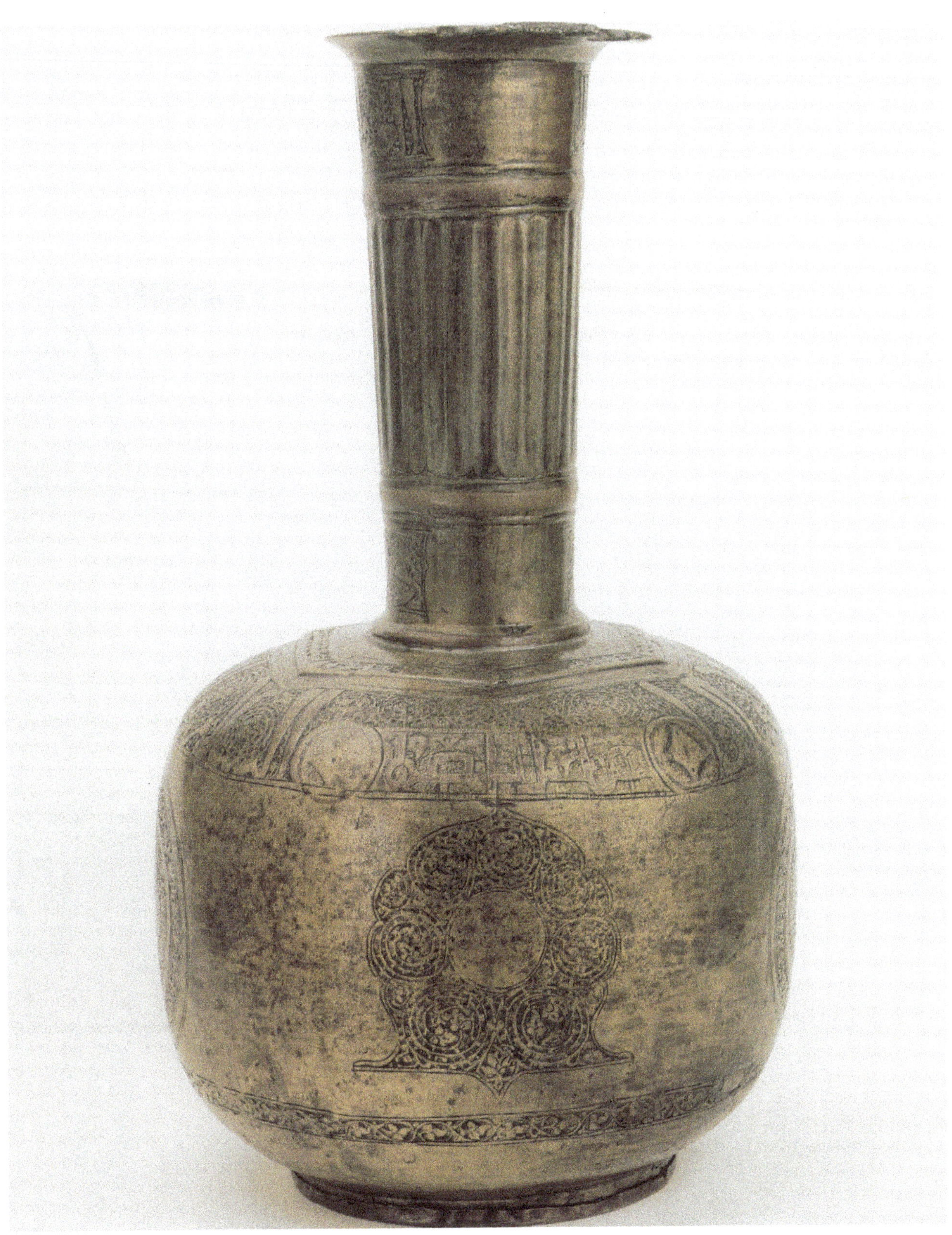

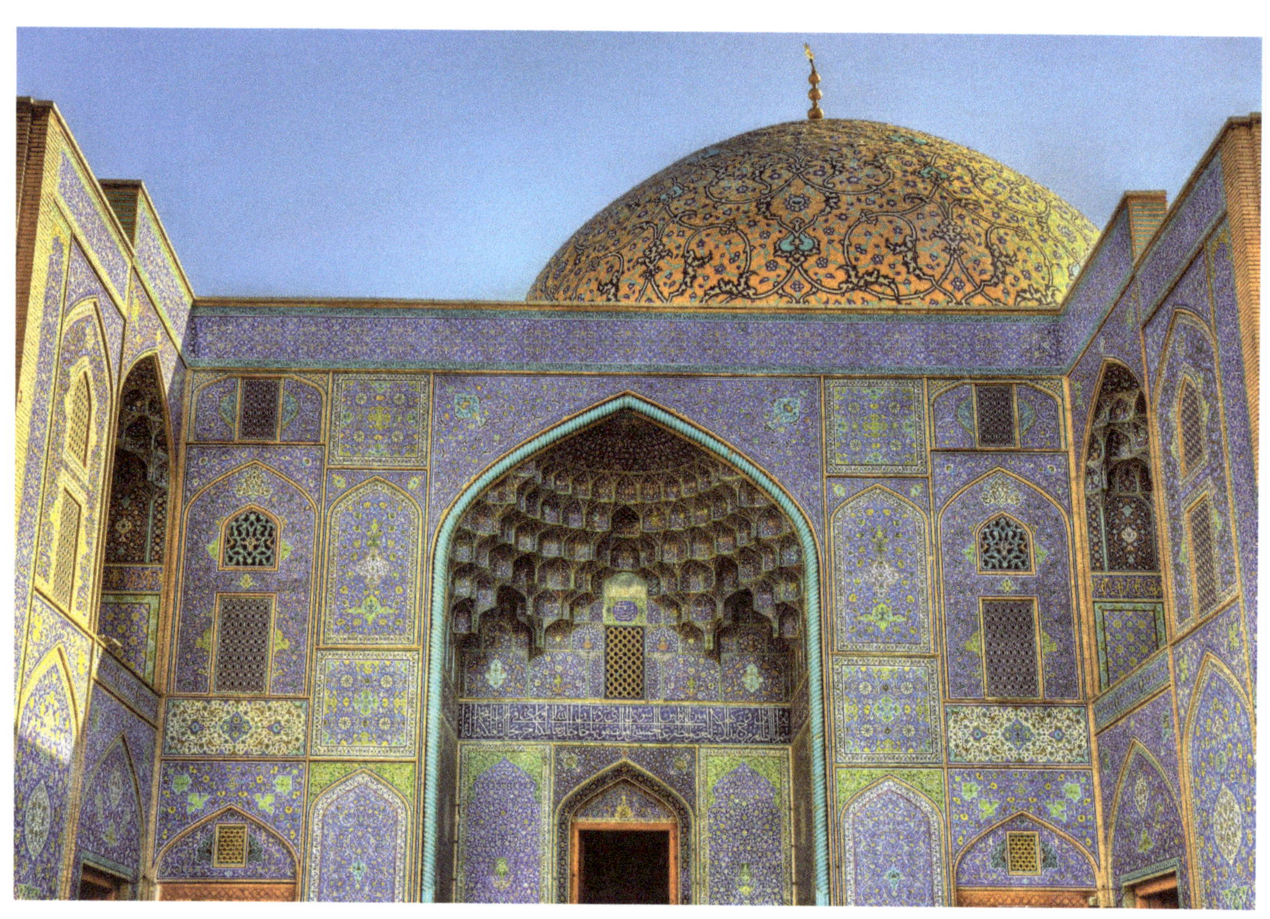

▲ Sheikh Lotfollah Mosque on Naqsh-e Jahan Square of Isfahan Iran

within it was not in terms of estates or between the nobility and the oppressed, but in terms of Muslims and infidels. In artistic terms, this social system fostered the creation not only of a hierarchy of forms and themes but also of a hierarchy of individual types of art. The Islamic conquest swept away the social system of castes and estates and in so doing significantly changed the hierarchy in subject matter and the branches of the fine arts. The Sassanian royal and "chivalric" culture was destroyed.

The Islamic conquest swept away a number of restrictions within Iranian culture, and not only religious ones but also those relating to estates. The Zoroastrian or state propagandist interpretations were eliminated from all artistic forms, themes and compositions which had been developed in Sassanian Iran; kings finally became simply kings; heroes, warriors and hunters simply themselves; beasts, birds, flowers and plants simply beasts, birds, flowers and plants. And this repertory, which included a great number of images and compositions imported from other cultures, passed into the art of medieval Iran, developing along the same general lines which characterized medieval art, such as an intensification of decoration and a striving towards abstract compositions.

And yet the art and culture of Iran did not fuse into a general Islamic culture. On the contrary, after the Iranian renaissance (10th-11th centuries) the Modern Persian language became the language of Islam together with Arabic and under the influence of the Iranians, Islam itself became a multilingual, multinational culture and religion.

From the 7th-9th centuries the eastern province of Iran, Khurasan, was of special significance in the founding of the new culture (in the Middle Ages it encompassed the north-east of present-day Iran, the south of present-day Turkmenistan and the north-west of present-day Afghanistan).

One immediate consequence of the Arab conquest of Iran was an influx of Arabs settling in many cities or setting up military camps which soon became cities. This Arab immigration was on a mass scale; in the 10th century, for example, the Arab population already constituted a majority in the city of Qum.

The second consequence was the spread of Islam and of Arabic. During the first two centuries of Islam in the territory of Khurasan, the religion of the Arabs underwent an intensive process of transformation into the religion of the entire Caliphate, whilst the language of the Koran and various Arab tribes developed into an Arab literary language; in all of this the Persians, who had converted to Islam, played no small part. It was here that Shi'ism, one of Islam's most important movements, developed, and in particular its extreme faction, Ismailism.

There was yet another important consequence of the change of power. Before the Abbasid age, the Islamic community of Iran had consisted primarily of Arabs and only afterwards of Persians converted to Islam. They did not possess equal rights with true Arabs. The Abbasids ended this division and in the same period many dihqans, who had preserved or even raised their social status, adopted Islam.

The creation of Modern Persian literature was a factor of the utmost importance for medieval Persian art, for it was this which was to serve as the basis of figurative art. The essential preconditions already existed: the illustrative quality and the variety of forms within late Sassanian art, the rich artistic traditions of wall painting in eastern Iran and Central Asia and the no less rich traditions of Christian art in the eastern provinces of Byzantium.

Mention must be made of the fundamental difference between the medieval art of Europe and that of Iran. In western medieval art prior to the Renaissance, the acts of God, the saints and ascetics formed the subject of man's "visual" impression of the world and of its morality and history; in the medieval art of the East, however, during the course of this entire period man himself and his acts became the main focus.

During the Middle Ages, the range of subjects in western art was universal, that of Persian art was national. This was a consequence of the fact that Iranian fine art was extremely closely linked to written and oral literature whose basic protagonists were ancient Iranian epic heroes and rulers, lovers, warriors, famous poets, and only very occasionally prophets and holy men.

At the time of the formation of the Caliphate and the emergence of Islam as its religion, it was natural that works of art from the preceding historical phase, such as metalwork, carved seals, stucco decoration, coins and silk textiles, should not change their range of subjects and motifs. The first Arab rulers minted coins on the Sassanian pattern, simply using the stamp for a Sassanian drachma with the addition of the Muslim religious formula "in the name of Allah" on the coin's face and, moreover, depicting themselves in the regalia of a Sassanid king of kings.

On the whole, it can be said that Persian art of the 8th-11th centuries was, first of all, unusually varied as regards its range of themes and subjects and its influences. It is true that there were attempts to create specific styles at the courts of rulers, such as a court style in Khurasan under al-Mamun (early 9th century) and under Mahmud of Ghazni (early 11th century), but these were merely episodes not leading to any sort of lasting unification.

Such variety is characteristic of all types of art at this time. In the architecture of Iran, for example, the hypostyle plan was introduced as the basic mosque layout, brought by the Arabs from the West, but at the same time the so-called "kiosk mosques" were being built, based on the Zoroastrian plan of the chahar taq, and tower mausoleums were spreading. Mosques were decorated with stucco panels consisting of plant and geometrical motifs, whilst in the east of the Islamic world, as in Nishapur, these motifs are extraordinarily close to those used in the west, for example in Iraq. At the same time we know of stucco panels of that period (mid-8th century, Chal-Tarkhan) which depict not only Sassanian animals but even Sassanian deities (Mithras on a stag) and heroes of Sassanian legends.

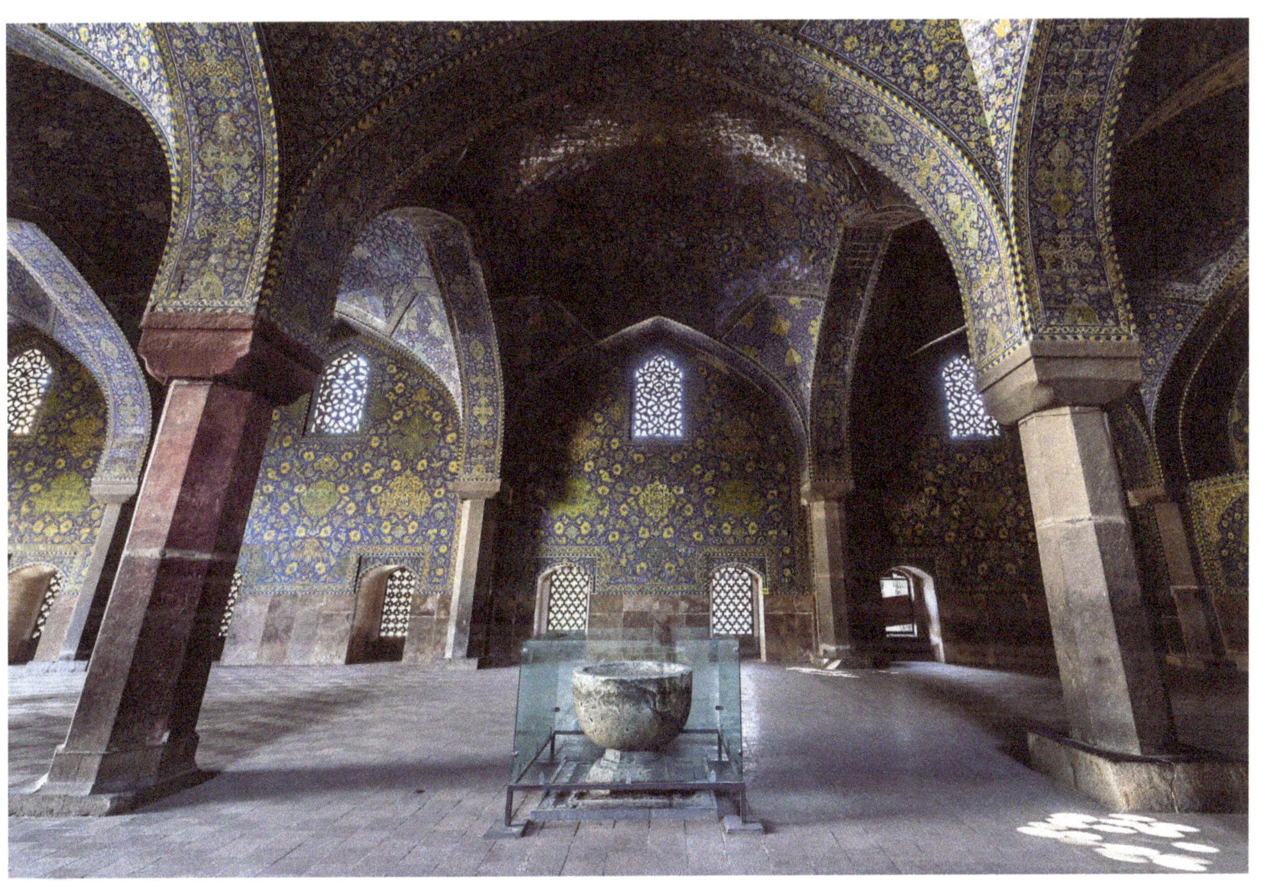

▲ Interior of Shah Mosque also called Imam mosque in Isfahan city Iran

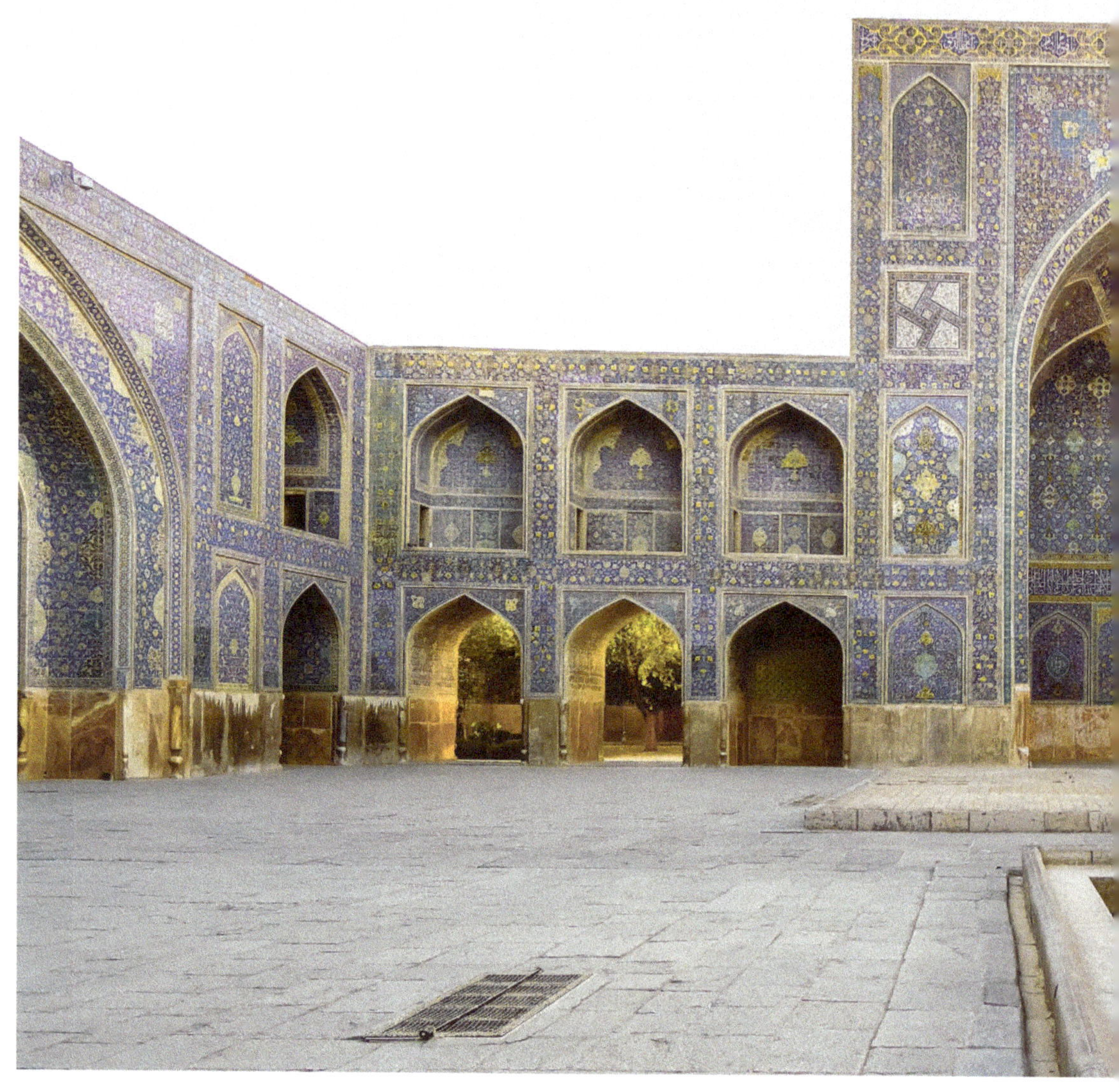

▲ View on Shah Mosque in Isfahan Iran

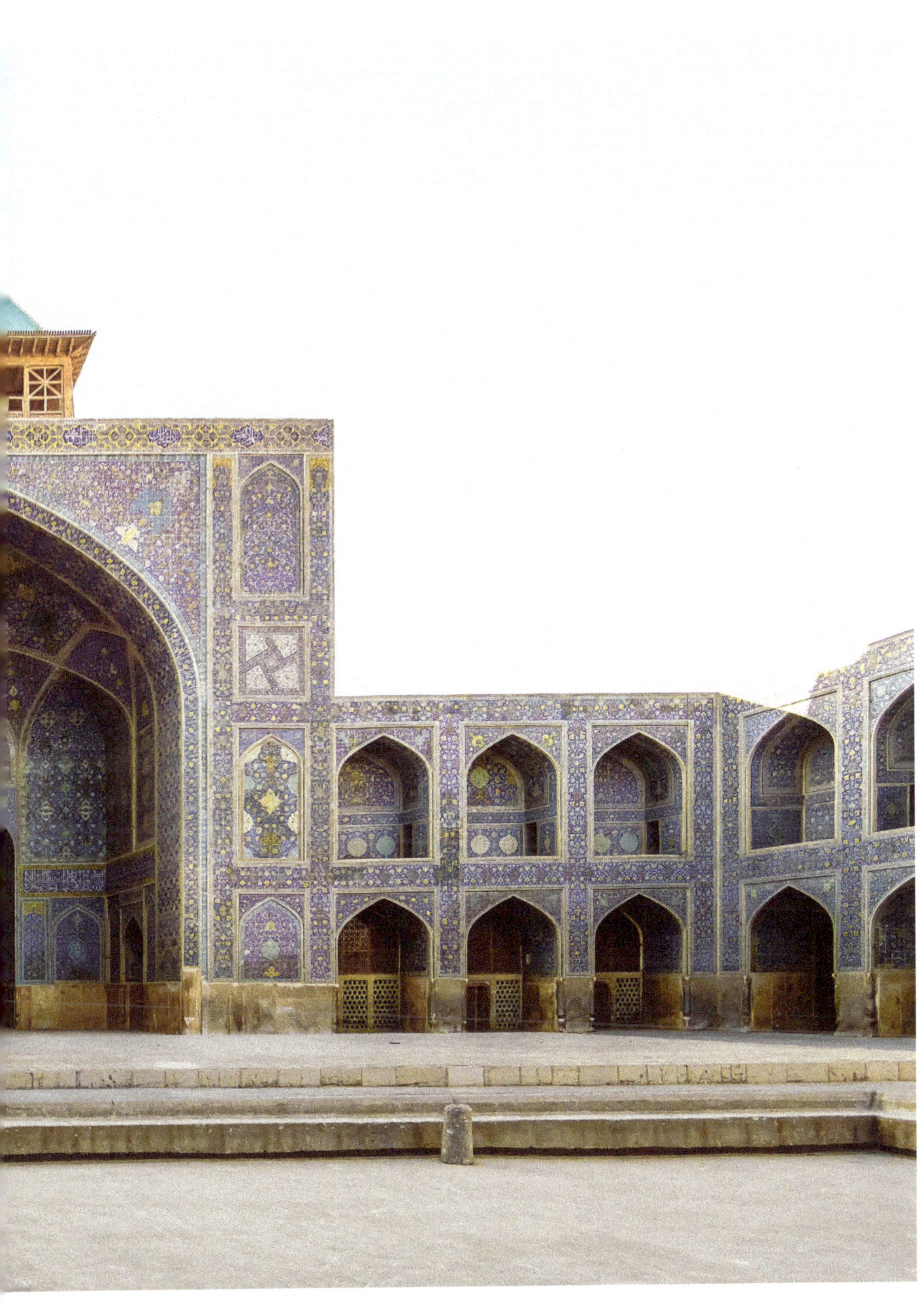

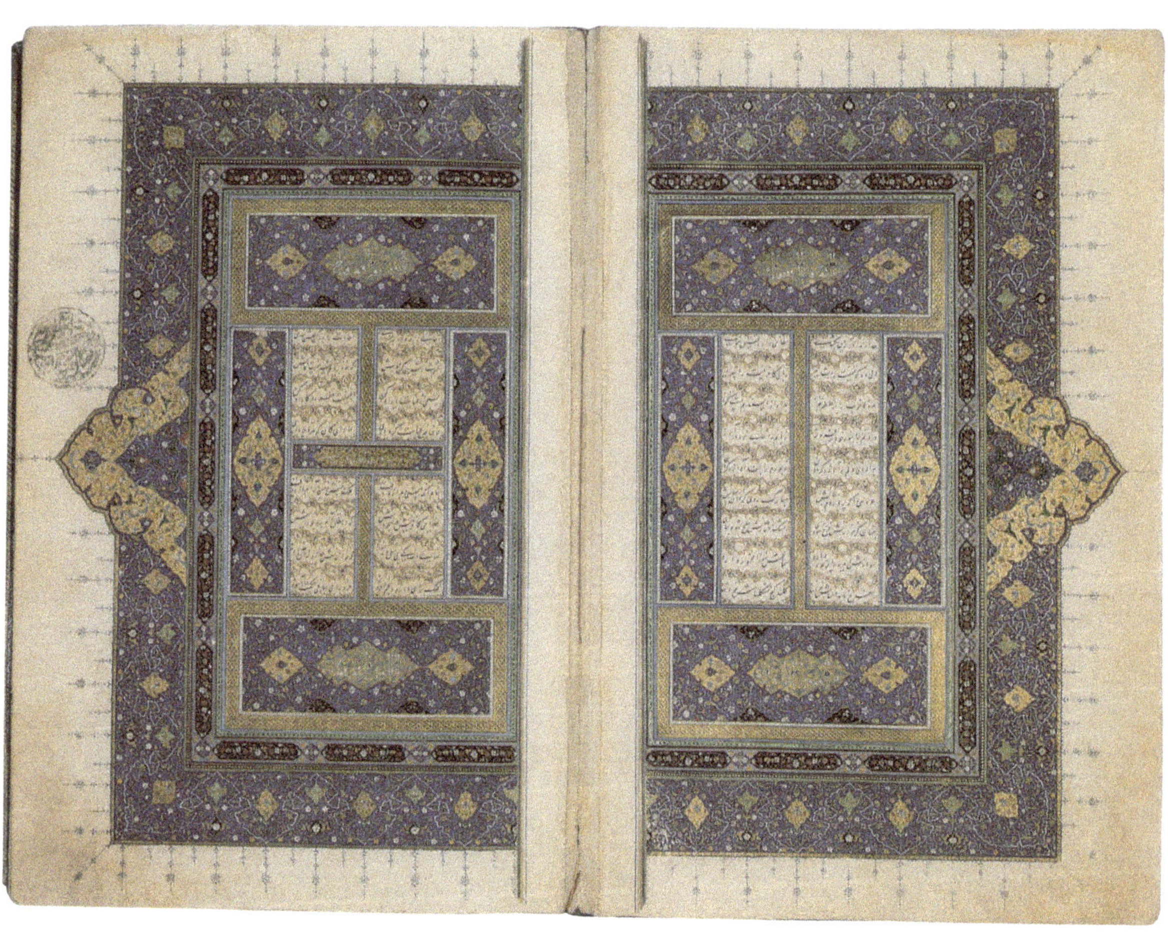

It is especially important that in the same period one sees how the propagandistic and class character of the hunt, feast and battle scenes have entirely disappeared – they have become standard scenes, lacking any significant meaning. Sassanian symbols degenerated into purely visual motifs. The same thing happened to Sassanian depictions of birds, beasts and plants. Although they only had a benedictory significance even in late Sassanian art, during the 8th-10th centuries they become mere ornamentation.

Strange new motifs appear during the 9th and early 10th centuries on Nishapur ceramics, and there alone. The designs portray birds, beasts, various monsters, horses being attacked by beasts of prey, dancers, figures in rich clothing holding goblets and flowers, and riders on horseback. All these designs do, of course, have their prototypes in Sassanian art, but they are very primitively executed with no regard for proportion and are sometimes mere caricatures. This ceramic style, which appeared suddenly and vanished just as suddenly, possibly in the course of a single century, is an example of those completely new aspects of art appearing in connection with the new discoveries.

◀ Frontispiece of a manuscript.
Late 1520s–early 1530s
35 x 24cm (opening). Manuscript: Khusrau and Shirin of Nizami. Calligrapher: Sultan Muhammad Nur. Date of completion of copy: 937 AH/1530–31 AD, Herat.
The National Library of Russia, St Petersburg.
Inv. No. Dom 346, f. 1b-2v.

From the beginning of the 11th century changes in Persian art are clearly distinguishable and this new phase covers a lengthy period of about 300 years, until the mid-14th century. It should be noted that ceramics and metalwork depicted the most vivid figurative images of this period. The golden age of miniature painting dates from around the end of this phase of Persian art (after the Mongol conquest) and this form was subsequently to occupy a dominant position in figurative art.

The political history of this period involves the rise of the Turkic dynasties of the Ghaznavids in the east and of the Seljuks, and the crushing Mongol conquest. In view of the fact that works of art have as yet been insufficiently researched it is impossible to relate them precisely to historical events.

In essence, the art of this period should not be termed a "renaissance" in the generally accepted sense of the word, since one can hardly consider its aim to have been the rebirth of old traditions. One thing is indisputable – the 11th to the mid-14th centuries represent the golden age of art in Iran. In architecture, for example, mosques on the four-iwan plan appear and spread throughout Iran. Whichever way they are interpreted, they are truly Iranian and for many centuries were the glory of Iranian architecture. We need name only such classical monuments as the minaret of Jam, the mosques of Isfahan, the mausoleum of Sanjar, the mosque of Varamin and others. Significant changes also occurred in metalwork.

Sassanian traditions still survived at this time and partly on this basis, though to a much greater extent on the basis of eastern Iranian traditions, processes came about which led to the formation of a new phase in art. This phase was to reach its zenith in the 15th century.

The most outstanding mosques of this time are the Isfahan mosques built between c. 1130-1150; the most outstanding mausoleums are those in Khwasan and Azerbaijan from the 12th-13th centuries; the most sophisticated ceramics are those of Rayy and Kashan, whilst the bronze inlay was produced predominantly in Khurasan.

Lusterware

No dynastic art of any sort was created. The art of Iran at this period was the art of cities, of cultural centers, an art of master craftsmen, calligraphers and painters scattered throughout the country, an art for various customers – for the sultan, of course, but also for the merchants and wealthy citizens. Possibly the most exciting branch of art of the 12th to mid-14th centuries was the production of ceramic vessels and tiles. At that time, the technique of manufacturing lusterware was becoming widespread.

The luster technique originated in Egypt as early as the 8th. Some scholars suggest that the secret of luster was actually imported into Iran by Egyptian potters who had moved from Cairo to Rayy after the fall of the Fatirnid dynasty (1171). The first precisely dated piece of Iranian lusterware is a jug from 1179 (The British Museum, London).

A vessel in The Metropolitan Museum of Art is the first in the hafl rang technique which, apart from its date (1187), also mentions the name of the artist, Abu Zayd al-Kashani. The style of painting on this vessel definitely has a number of connections with the Mosul School of miniatures. But the people depicted on it are generally "moon-faced", as the poets wrote with narrow eyes and a small mouth; their hair, sometimes even that of the men, is braided into plaits and falls to their shoulders; their heads are, as a rule, surrounded by halos. Its emergence coincides with the arrival in Iran of the Seljuk Turks, and the closest surviving parallel for these portrayals is provided by the Manichaean wall paintings of Turfan.

A number of literary subjects are found on ceramics and tiles. Sometimes they are well known. The entire range of objects allows one to construct a certain albeit sketchy, picture of Iranian figurative art over this period.

It has its standard themes (the royal banquet, the hunt, throne scenes, battles) founded on a tradition

Vase. ▶
Second half of 13th century
Faience, painted in lustre; double firing. Height 80cm.
The Hermitage, St Petersburg.
Inv. No. IR-1595.
Acquired 1885 from the V. Bazilevsky collection.

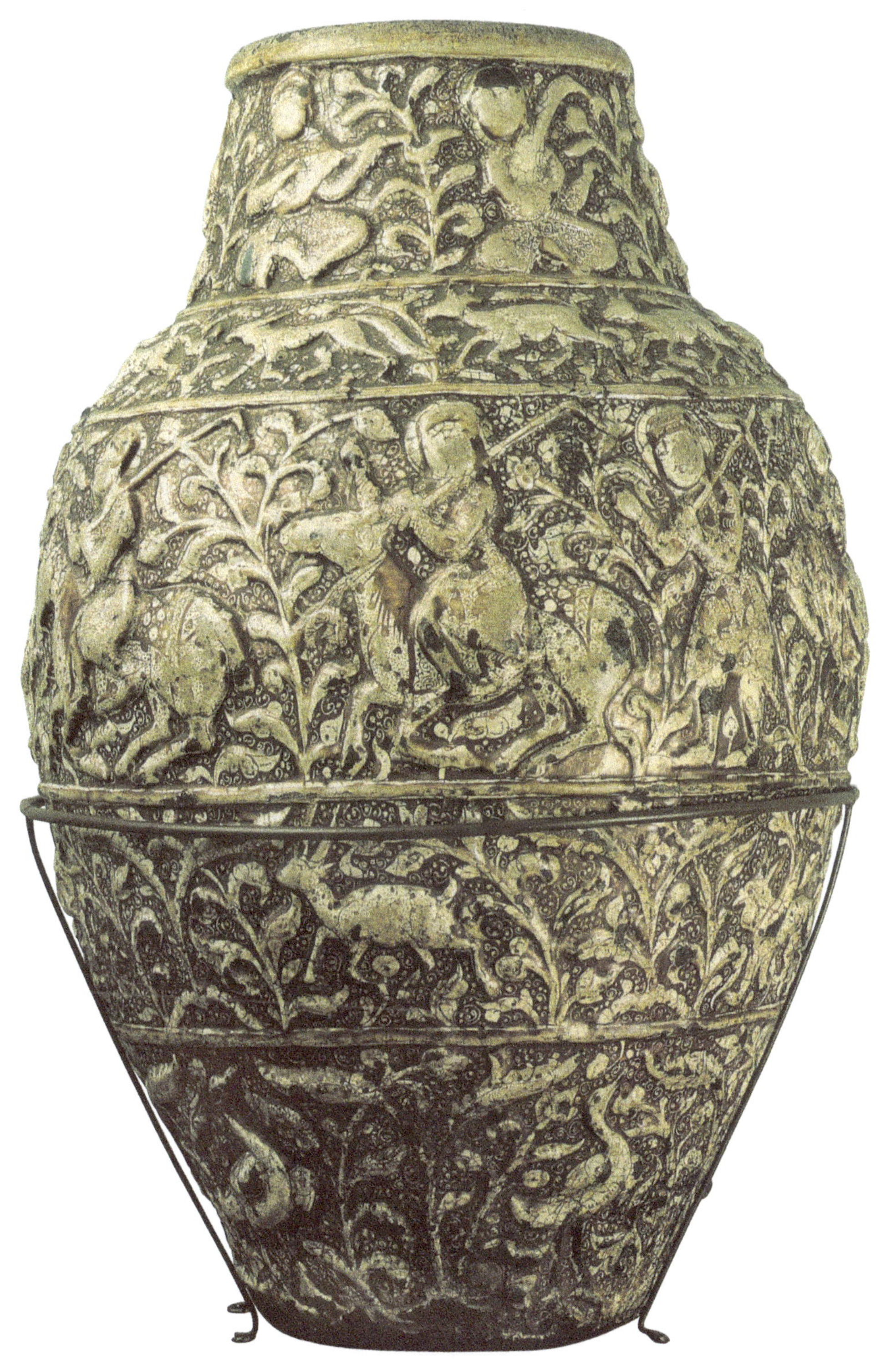

وی ازین جهان مفارقت کرده باشند از ذکر باری تعالی خالی مبو و پیوسته کسی ازیشان بقان

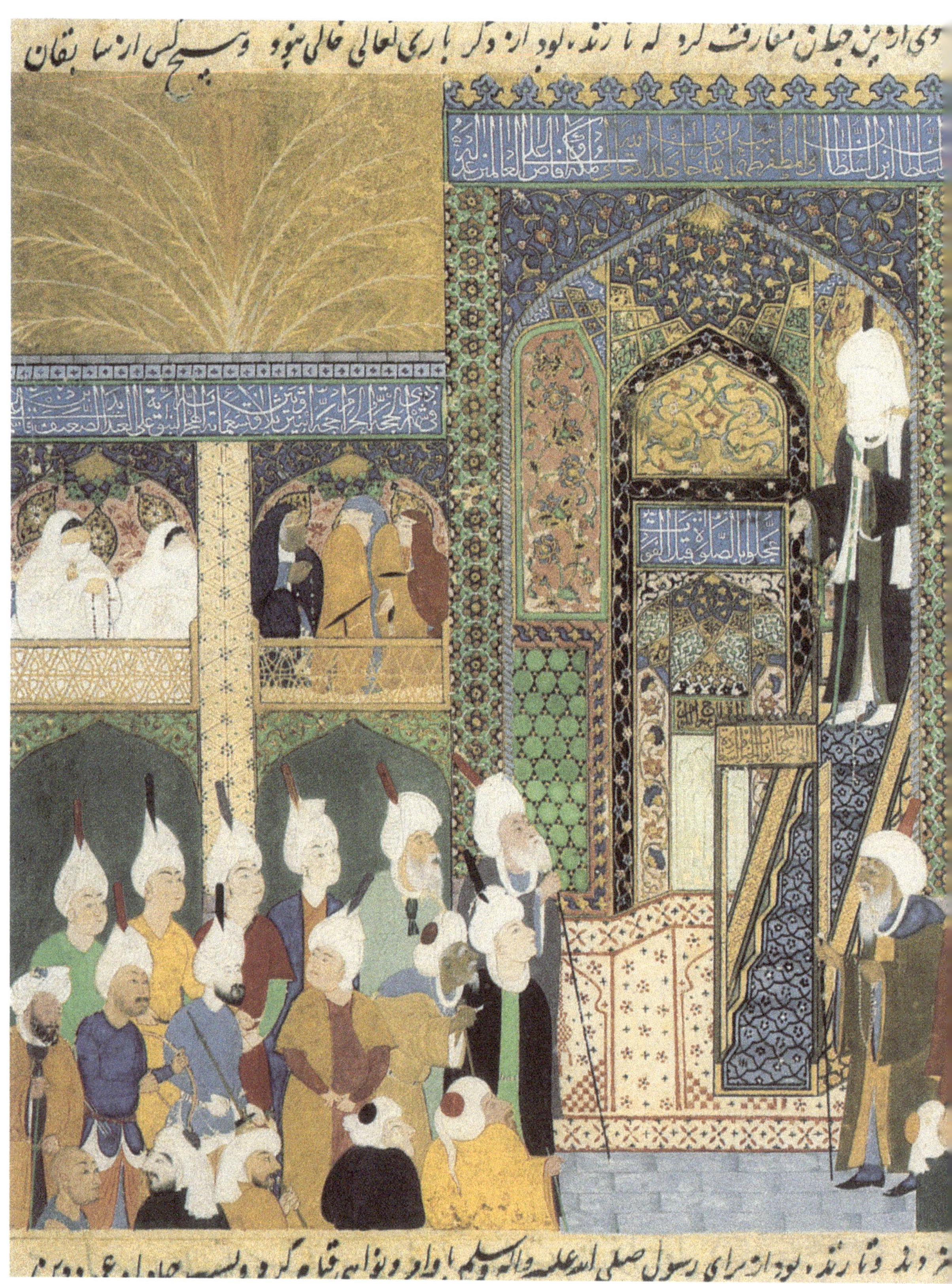

مرده وتارند بود ازبرای رسول صلی الله علیه واله سلم اواد ونواله ثناه کرده ولسبه جاه ا۱ ۶۰۰۰ م

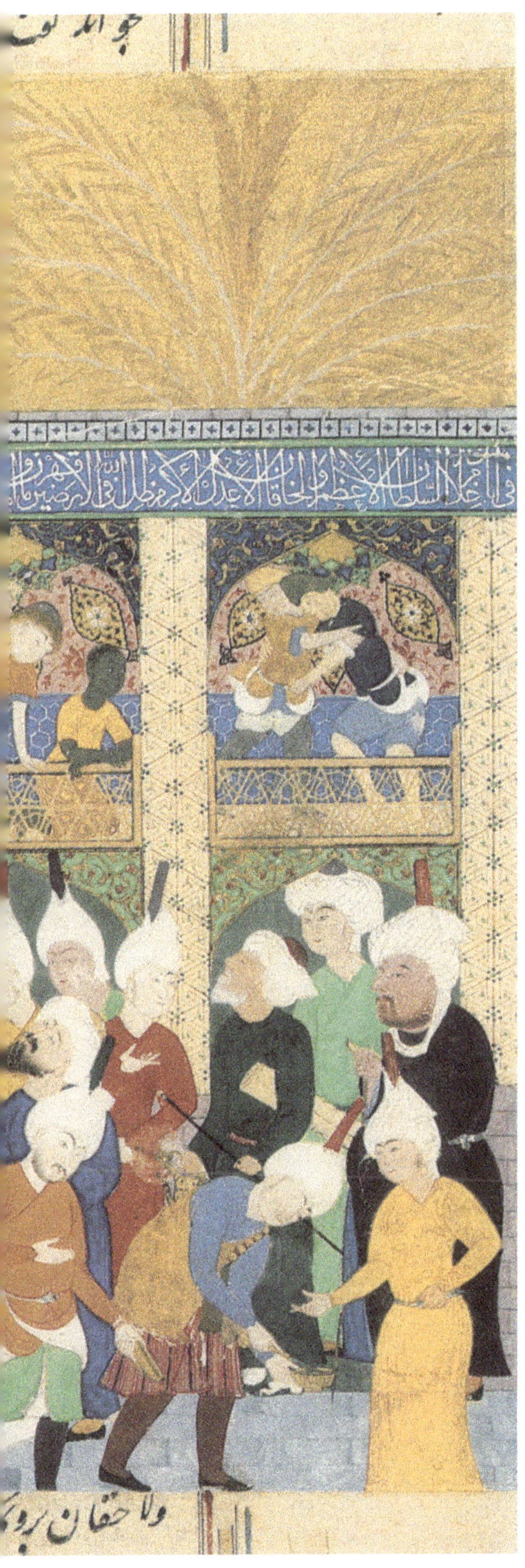

of great antiquity, but generalized and lacking any individual traits. These subjects are entertaining stories of ancient heroes and kings, of love and life's pleasures, etc. One also finds extremely rich ornamentation: flowers, trees, fruit, birds and beasts, often of a standard type and serving as a background or even as an independent subject, although still remaining ornamental.

The craftsman praises his work, glorying in his art. Illustration overwhelms the object: even the letters of the inscription are formed with their tips in the shape of human or animal heads or simply in the form of fighting warriors (for example, on the famous early 13th-century bronze goblet in the Cleveland Museum of Art).

The works themselves cease to be anonymous. The craftsmen who made them sometimes added their names to the object and the date when it was completed, as did the scribes of manuscripts and their illustrators. They often used the standard formula: "Such and such a craftsman painted this." This signifies that he applied both the inscription and the design to the object.

◀ Miniature: The First Sermon of Hasan ibn Ali.
By Qasim ibn Ali. Dhu-l-hijja 932 AH/September 1526 AD.
21 x 15.8cm. Manuscript: Ahsan al-Kibar of Muhammad al-Husaini al-Varamini. Calligrapher: Khizr-shah.
Date of completion of copy: 4 Rabi' 1837 AH/19 October 1433 AD.
The National Library of Russia, St Petersburg.
Inv. No. Dorn 312, f. 373b.

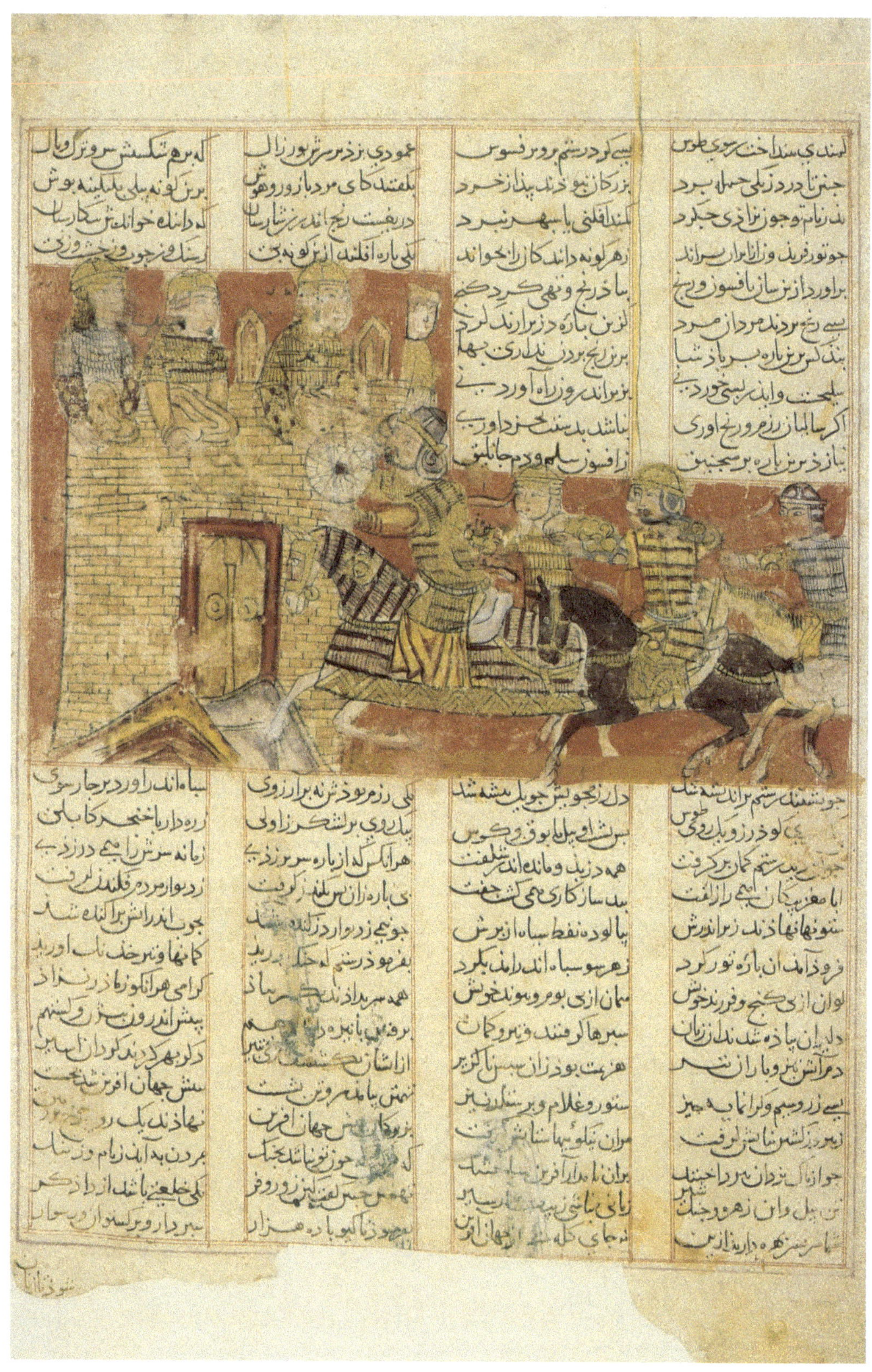

PERSIAN MANUSCRIPT ILLUMINATION AND PERSIAN MINIATURE PAINTING

At this point it is necessary to look more closely at the history of Persian manuscript illumination. The first Persian manuscript with real miniatures that is known to us is the Persian poem of Ayyuqi, Varqah and Gulshah, commonly assigned to the early or mid-13th century. It was probably produced in Upper Mesopotamia (Jazira) or Anatolia.

The miniatures were painted by the artist Abd al-Mumin ibn-Muhammad al-naqqash al-Khowi. The frieze-like compositions of several miniatures are analogous to frescos, with the interrupted action continuing beyond the frame in a linear development; some of them are painted against a vivid, often deep red background, which is characteristic of frescos and also of the miniatures

of the Kyzyl Manichaean treatise; absolutely every detail of iconography and style in this group of miniatures coincides with those found on contemporary lusterware, exactly as on ceramics.

It is the influence of the Iranian miniature which is adduced to explain the illustrations on metalwork and even the style of painting of Iranian ceramics. But is there any evidence at all, even circumstantial, bearing witness to the existence of miniature painting in Iran during the period before the end of the 13th century? We do have a manuscript treatise on astronomy, Abd al-Rahman al-Sufi's Book of the Fixed Stars, completed in 1009-1010 CE.

It contains fine drawings and scientific illustrations which are of a set type and are treated exactly like all illustrations to scientific works of the time. These are not, of course, miniatures in the true sense of the word; they lack any artistic perception of the world.

Even earlier accounts are just as sparse and imprecise. There are the accounts of the already mentioned "official portraits" of the Sassanid rulers in the book of Sassanian history, and there is the information that the collection of fables, Kalila and Dimna, translated in the 8th century from Middle Persian into Arabic, had been illustrated by Chinese artists. All other reports speak not of early Iranian manuscript illumination but of portrait painting or scientific illustration.

We have already seen that the portrait miniature as a genre had already established itself in the Sassanian period, and developed, even flourished, in Iranian painting during the following centuries.

Thus the facts available at present attest that fresco painting existed on Iranian territory in the 10th-12th centuries, and that it was above all widespread in the north-east and beyond the borders of Iran; that portrait painting has been known in Iran since the Sassanian period; that there are a number of illustrations of literary and epic subjects on works of applied art, and even cycles of such illustrations, and finally, that the very earliest manuscript miniatures in Persian works known to us (Varqah and Gulshah and the Shiraz Shahnamas) bear witness to the influence of fresco paintings and the decoration of ceramics.

One can suggest that the illustrative, narrative quality, which had already been present for a long time in Persian art – in wall paintings, metalwork, stucco and textiles – became widespread during the 11th and 12th centuries in ceramics as well; only afterwards did those same artists also create Iranian manuscript illustrations. This is all the more likely, since one characteristic of Persian artistic perception is an extremely close connection between word and object, literature and fine art.

These miniatures differ fundamentally in their draftsmanship from what we are generally accustomed to seeing in later Persian miniatures (15th-17th centuries). In terms of their technique these miniatures are, on the one hand, connected to fresco painting and on the other, to paintings on ceramics of the so-called Rayy type, in which peculiarities of brushstrokes and contour are explained by technical demands.

The total silence of early Persian sources on the subject of manuscript illumination is strange. How many stories they tell of wall painting! And not a single reliable reference to Persian illuminated manuscripts or Persian miniaturists before the 14th century.

In the 14th century the feudal system was at its height in Iran. At the same time, from the middle of the century, it was the age of individual rulers each striving to create their own magnificent court, but these rulers were both weaker and poorer than their predecessors and there had long been no vast frescos in their palaces, no stucco panels depicting the heroic exploits of their noble ancestors and no portraits of themselves.

Miniature painting and calligraphy appear to have become the chief "prestigious" branches of art. Costly manuscripts of ancient narrative poems

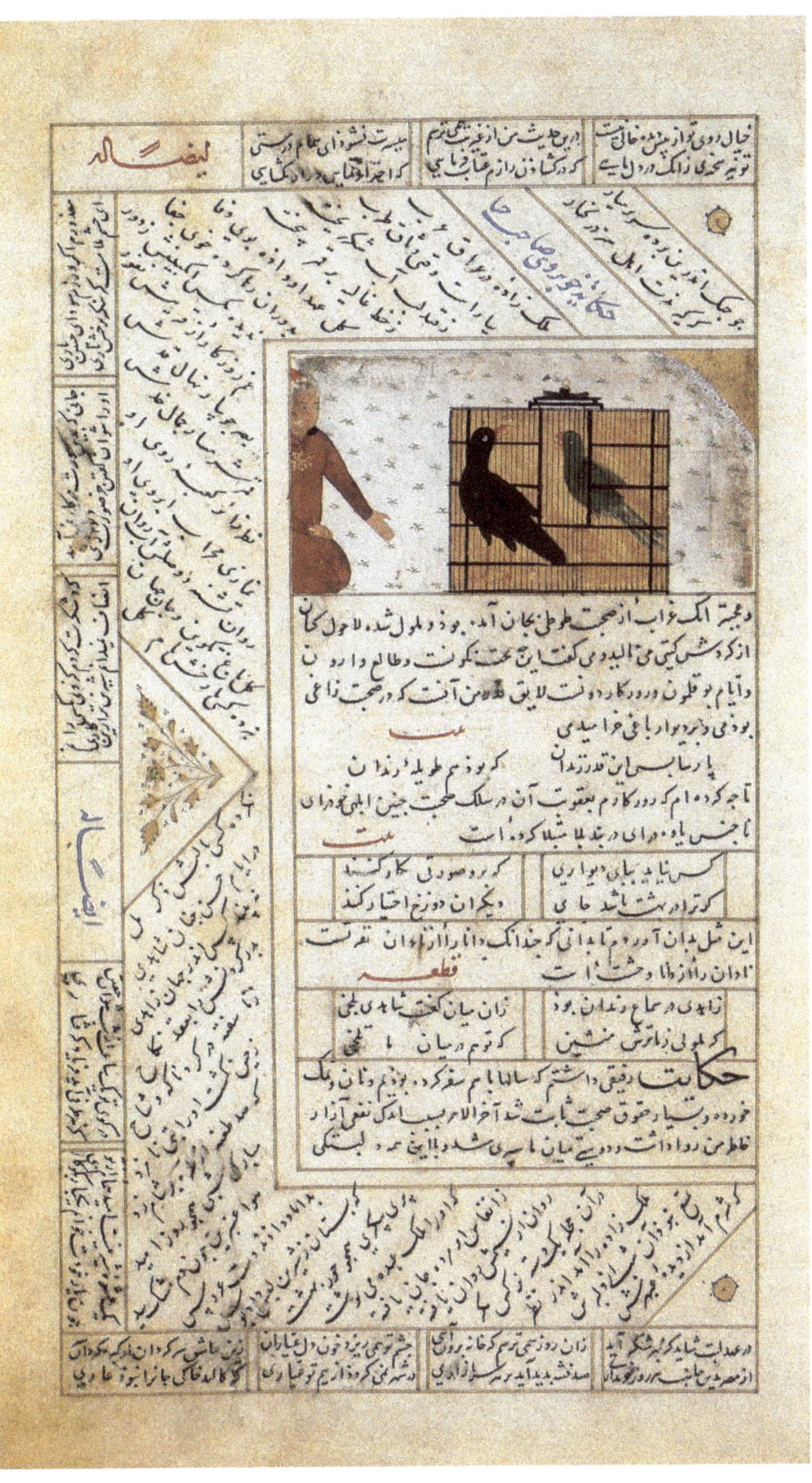

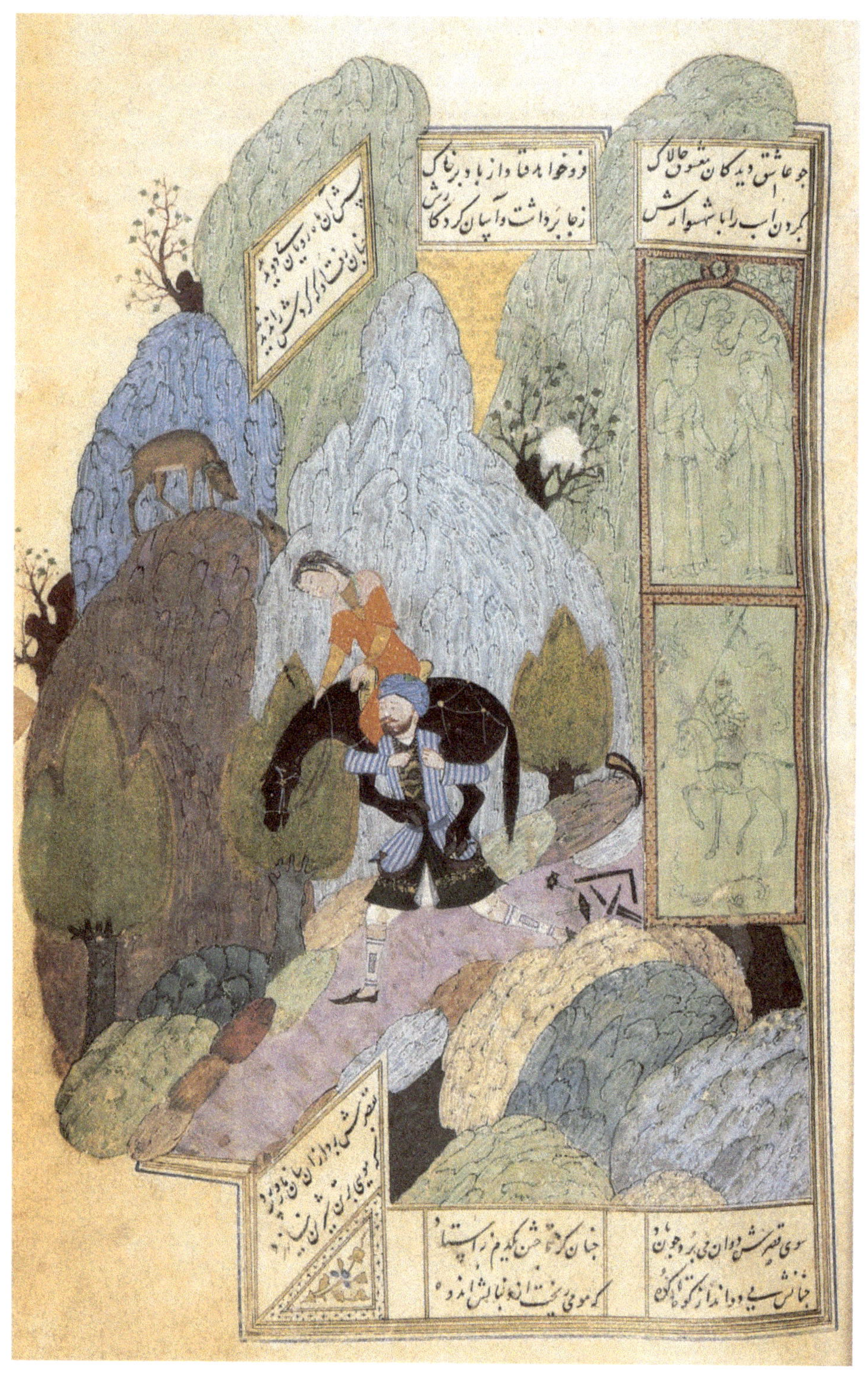

or verses written by the ruler's court poets or by historians praising his, or his ancestors', grandeur, and decorated with miniatures executed by court painters or simply by skilled miniaturists involved in commercial production were highly prized. As for ceramics and metalwork, they were "democratized".

Craftsmen produced these articles for the middle ranks of society. Thus, there were no longer ceramics bearing texts of great poems and decorated with pictures that were either themes from these poems or, much more frequently, pictorial equivalents of the verses. The social class of customers was changing and Persian miniature painting occupied the position of the most prestigious branch of art.

The previously mentioned Shiraz school of miniature painting is represented by illuminated manuscripts from the first decade of the 14th century onwards. Eight examples are known, four of them being Firdawsi's poem, the Shahnama. In the earliest copies, the miniatures are executed in a flat style with strong affinities to wall painting and painting on ceramic.

The large number of miniatures in these early manuscripts is interesting, but it is even more important to note that many of them are simple, standard compositions, such as scenes of a palace

◀ Miniature:
Farhad Carrying the Horse and Shirin. 1430s
16 x 12,1cm.
Manuscript: Khamsa of Nizami. 835 AH/1431 AD.
The Hermitage, St Petersburg.
Inv. No. VR-1000. Transferred 1924 from the museum
attached to the former Stieglitz School of Technical Design.

reception, a battle or various sorts of garden scenes or hunts. Thus, in the manuscript of the Shahnama dating from 1333, for example, out of 52 miniatures more than 30 are standard scenes of battles, hunts and "conversations".

Early miniatures are extremely exact illustrations of the text. Like those in medieval western manuscripts, they are based on a standard subject into which some significant concrete detail from the story they illustrate has been introduced. Therefore, when depicting Zahhak, the artist reproduced the standard scene of a king on a throne but added the snakes that grow from the king's shoulders.

Yet at the same period in Tabriz the masterpiece of Iranian illumination was produced, the Demotte Shahnama, which we have already mentioned. At that time the Mongol dynasty of the Ilkhans ruled in Tabriz. These were the descendants of the grandson of Genghis Khan. One of them, Ghazan Khan (1295-1304), attempting to rescue the country from the cruel devastation that had been a consequence of Mongol invasion and rule, announced a series of important official reforms which were put into practice by his vizier, Rashid al-Din.

Rashid al-Din's chief work, Jami al-tavarikh (Collection of Chronicles), is permeated by these concepts. The work was conceived as a genuinely universal history which would include the history of all the then known peoples, from the Franks to the Chinese. To realize this grandiose plan an entire "academy" was founded, which included scholars, calligraphers and artists – among them were two Chinese scholars, a Buddhist monk from Kashmir, a Catholic monk from France, scholars of Mongol traditions, etc. The manuscript of the Collection of Chronicles was illustrated by artists who strove to portray "ethnographic pictures" of the various peoples.

Not long afterwards a sumptuous manuscript of the Shahnama was produced, astounding in the quality of its miniatures and the originality of its approach. It has been suggested that the choice of themes for its 120 or more miniatures was governed by a definite program.

First of all, this program stressed the legitimacy of royal power, which alone provides the strength and might of a legitimate lord and his divine predestination to power. However, the important fact is that the miniatures are painted with overwhelming mastery; they are already far from being simply illustrations, although there are plenty of standard motifs in this Shahnama – throne scenes, hunts, banquets and battles. The miniatures of the Demotte Shahnama are the first to represent a new movement in Iranian miniature painting, one that has nothing to do with illustration, for "the elaboration of the narrative through the image of man leads the viewer to a highly moral interpretation of the epic". But the Demotte Shahnama is a unique manuscript that did not give rise to any imitations. In essence, the style of Iranian miniature painting was laid down in the 1360s and 1370s in the cities of Baghdad and Shiraz, and this was the style which was to determine its development for several centuries.

Around this time, the initial stage of development of Iranian miniature painting – the stage represented by the miniatures in Varqah and Gulshah or the

Shiraz Shahnamas of 1330 and 1333, or by the so-called "Small Shahnamas" of the same period – was gradually but inexorably becoming a thing of the past.

Chinese painting of the Sung period played an important role in establishing the new style, especially in the depiction of landscape. Motifs from Chinese ceramics and textiles, widespread in Iran at that time, were equally important. Contemporary Arab miniature painting and Rashidiyya miniatures also played a large part.

During this period, it was manuscripts of the Shahnama which were most often illustrated. At that time, the Shahnama was arousing interest, in effect for the first time since it had been written, evidently for political reasons, both at the Mongol Court of the Ilkhans and at the court of their vice-regents, the Injuids in Shiraz. The development of genres in Iranian miniature painting began with the illustration of this work, which was viewed at the time not from the angle of its poetical merits but above all from that of its legitimist ideas.

The best painters of the time, brought from Tabriz and Shiraz, were gathered in Herat. The literature, painting and calligraphy of Iran developed in kitabkhanah as those founded by Rashid al-Din and Baysunghur. As objects of pride to the rulers at whose courts they were founded, such kitabkhanah naturally reflected the tastes of their patrons and the actual problems of the day.

The existence of several schools of miniature painting at various times in Tabriz, Shiraz, Mashhad,

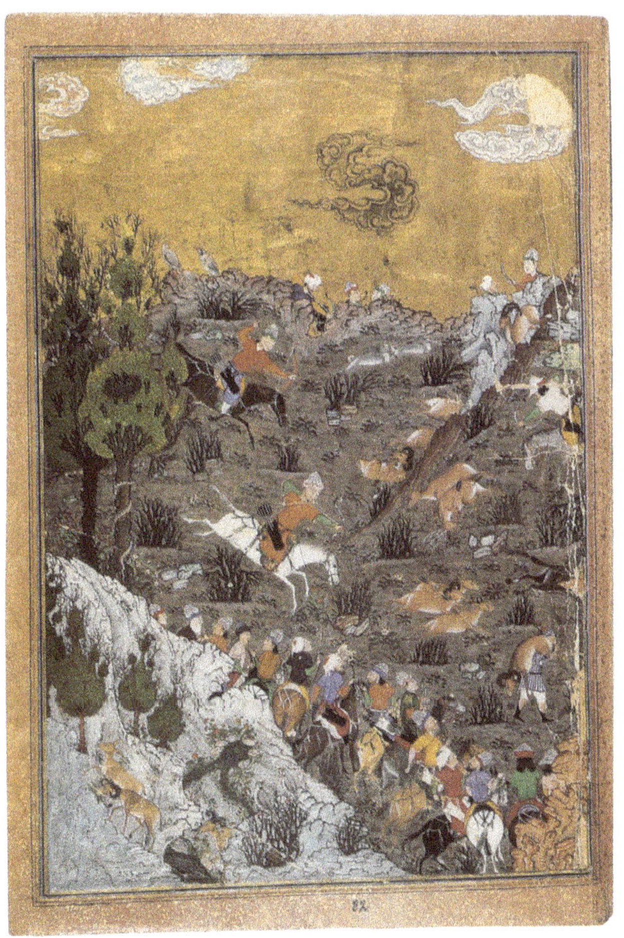

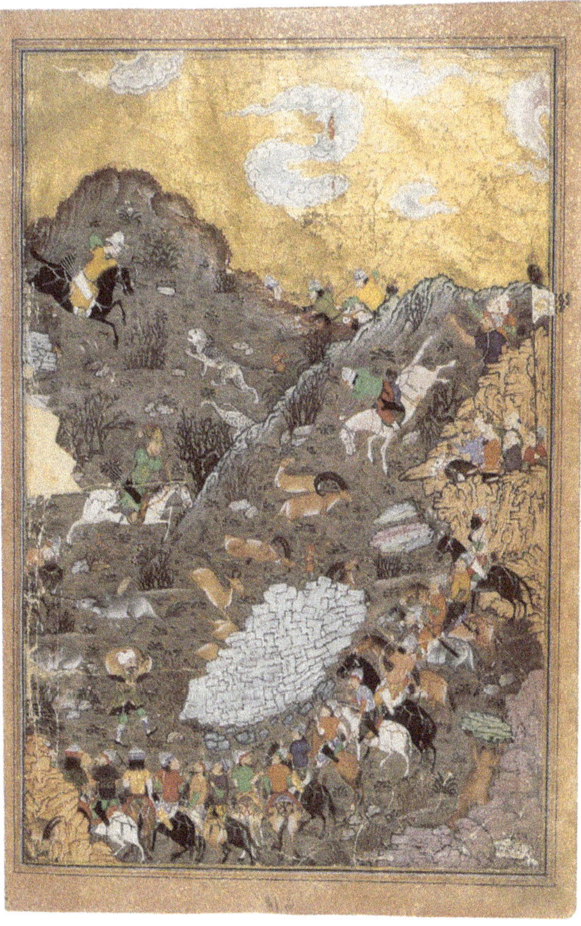

The Shah's Hunt. 1460s–1470s
27 x 37.5cm and 25.5 x 37.8cm.
Manuscript: Silsilat al-Dhahab of Jami. Date of
completion of copy: 1 Sha'ban 956 AH/25 August 1549
AD. Calligrapher: Shah-Mahmud al-Nishapuri.
The National Library of Russia, St Petersburg.
Inv. No. Dorn 434, f. 816-82a.

▼   Miniature: Portrait of a Girl.
By Riza-i Abbasi. 1011 AH/ 1602–03 AD
Indian ink, paints and gold on paper. 14.8 x 8.4cm
(19.3 x 16.9cm with borders). The Hermitage, St Petersburg.
Inv. No. VR-705. Acquired 1924 from the museum attached
to the former Stieglitz School of Technical Design.

▼   Youth Holding a Jug.
By Riza-i Abbasi, 1037 AH/ 1627–28 AD.12.5 x 22.3cm.
Museum of Western and Oriental Art, Kiev. Inv. No. 449 GRV.

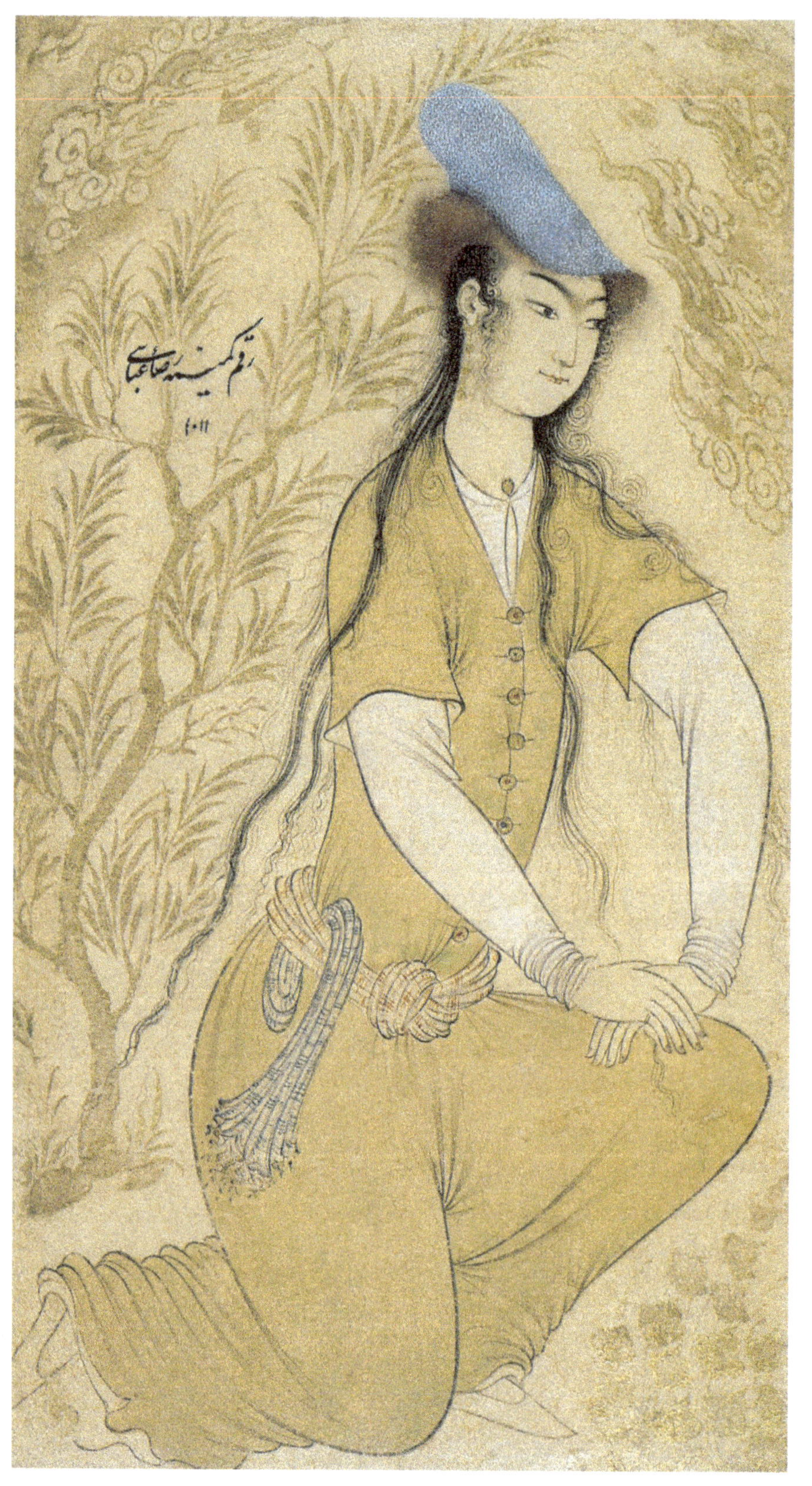

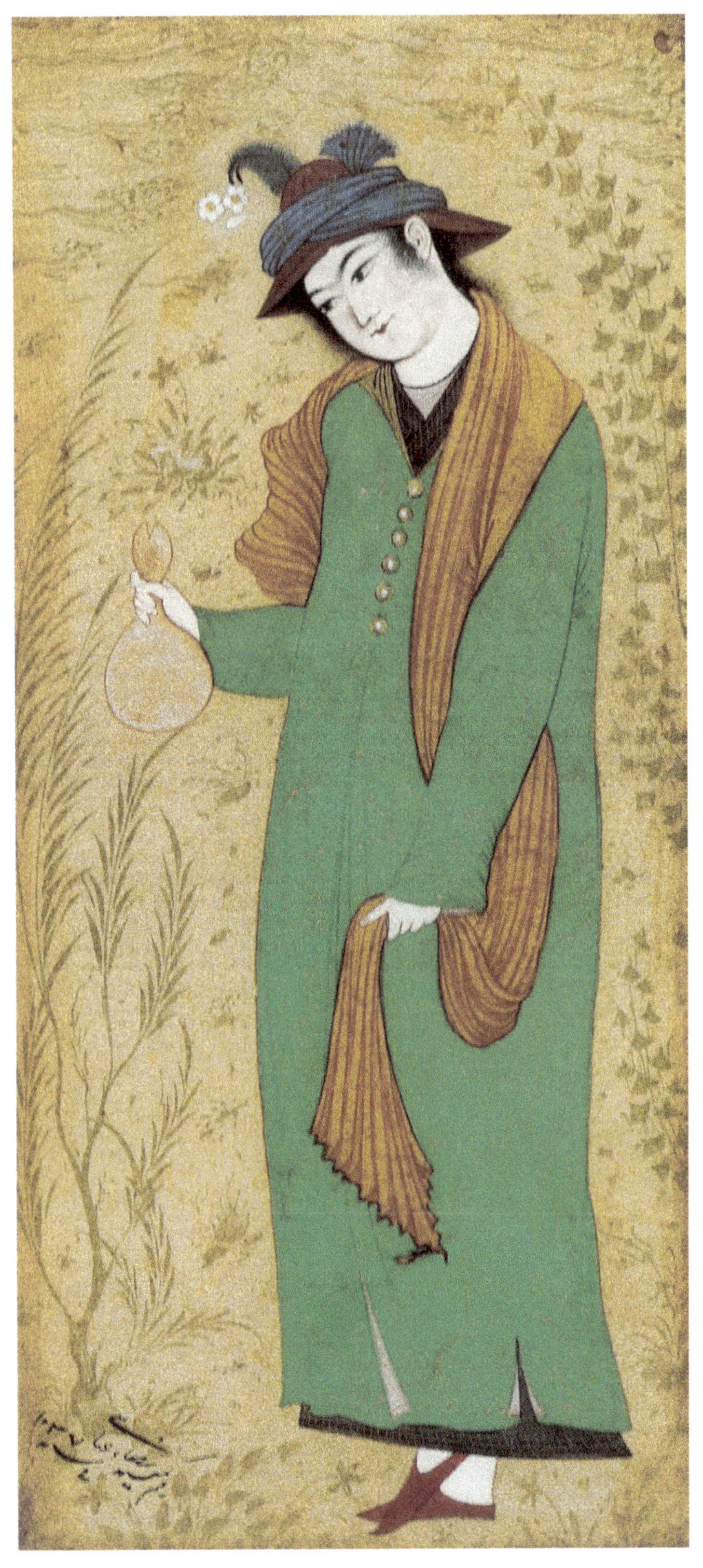

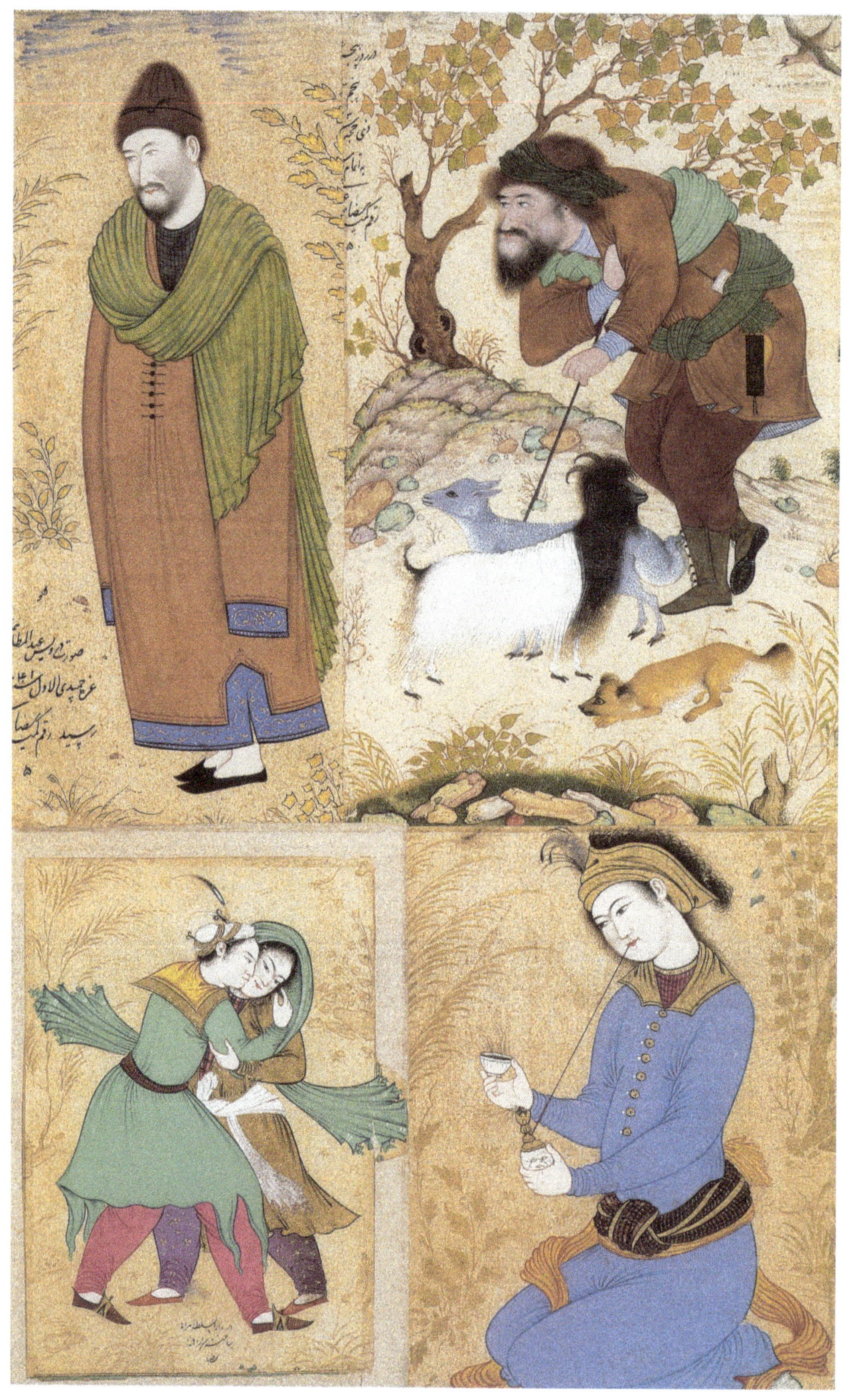

Isfahan has been established. These schools all passed through phases of flowering and decay. Thus, in the 15th to early 16th centuries, the Herat School reached the peak of achievement; in the 16th century miniature painting was dominated by the Tabriz school, and in the 17th by the Isfahan School.

The number of Persian verses on copper and bronze objects increases during the course of the 16th century. Arabic inscriptions meanwhile, especially benedictory ones, practically fall into disuse towards the beginning of the 16th century, but at the same time two new Arabic inscriptions appear, linked to the rise to power of the Safavid dynasty in Iran (1501-1736) – these are verses in honor of Ali and blessings on the Shi'ite imams, and they become prevalent on all types of object, in architecture and the applied arts. Thus, in the mid-14th century a new phase begins in the history of art in Iran. The transitional period probably lasts a fairly long time, more than fifty years. One feature which characterizes the art of this age is a loss of interest in the depiction of people on objects of applied art. This is indeed a surprising fact and one which has not yet been explained, for in this phase the Persian miniature flourished.

◄ Four miniatureson one sheet. By Riza-1 Abbasi

a. The Dervish Abd al-Mutallib Selmnani (?), 1 Jumada I 1041 AH/ 25 November 1631 AD. 7.3 x 16.4cm.
b. A Shepherd. 25 Dhu-l-hijja 1043 AH/22 June 1634 AD. 10.4 x16.4cm.
c. Love Scene. 1610s–1620s. 7.4 x 10.4cm.
d. Youth with a Hookah. 1610s–1620s. 8.8 x 12cm.

The National Library of Russia, St Petersburg.
Inv. No. Dom 489, f. 73b.

We now see a renewal of interest in representations of the human form, which is probably most clearly visible in textiles, although one may suppose that such fabrics do not represent a large proportion of the entire range of textile production. In 17th-century ceramics the strong influence of Chinese art can again be observed, but now aroused by the interest of Europeans in Chinese porcelain.

During this phase, active contact with European art begins – first of all in painting. Traces of European influence can already be observed in the mid-17th century. First and foremost, this influence involves the court miniature, but it then spreads to other branches of art where it is reflected to varying degrees. It is important to stress the fact that interest in European art initially arose in court circles.

Although there are few precisely dated pieces from the late 17th and early 18th centuries, a chronological series can be reconstructed. Changes are noticeable which could be explained by a decline in the quality of pieces, linked to their increased mass production. For example, on copper and bronze items, the surface of the background to the design is not entirely hatched. The omission of the hatching increases during the first half of the 18th century and around the middle of the century a complete break with tradition takes place, for in the second half of the century the background of Iranian copper and bronze objects is tooled with punches and the hatching disappears completely.

The great changes in the decoration of metalwork also paralleled in the other applied arts. During the first half of the 18th century the characteristic scrolled tendril in the background of the inscription on 17th-century seals either degenerates into a few small spirals or disappears entirely. The character of the writing also changes gradually: letters become thicker especially where they curve. This process culminates in the 19th century.

The fall of the Safavid dynasty seems to mark the end of the development of late Iranian ceramics, around c. 1720-1730. There is a clear boundary, expressed in the decline of technical skill – the objects are overloaded with decoration, the cobalt and luster painting is of poor quality – which distinguishes even late Safavid faience from late 18th- and early 19th-century ceramics.

An abrupt alteration in the style of miniatures occurs in the second half of the 17th century, linked to the influence of European painting and, possibly, to that of the Indian miniature. The style of the Isfahan School of miniatures, known to us in the work of Riza-i Abbasi, survives until the beginning of the 18th century, but then vanishes completely. Thus, one can assume that a new period begins in the history of Iranian painting at the turn of the 18th century; a new style immediately becomes prevalent in lacquer ware also. As far as the history of architecture is concerned, we can draw a line between the 17th and the 18th-19th centuries. Some changes also occurred here, possibly throughout the 18th century.

Thus, we can state with some confidence that at the end of the 17th century Persian art entered a period of change, heralding the beginning of a new phase. Evidently the first half of the 18th century is a sort of transitional period and new elements are finally victorious in the mid-18th century.

Unfortunately, the new phase begins with a "dark age" characterized by a decline in technical skills. This was reflected in all aspects of applied art in Iran, in ceramics, metalwork, carpets and textiles, but was not caused by any great social crisis in society; rather it was a result of the collapse of life in the cities where crafts were concentrated, largely as a result of the extremely unstable political situation in the country. Wars and invasions brought desolation and ruin to the cities in the second half of the 18th century and at the very beginning of the 19th century.

Turning to the new phase which began during the middle of the 18th century, we are treading on extremely unstable ground, composed of assumptions and hypotheses, for not a single aspect of the art of that time has yet been researched. Generally speaking, interest in 19th-century Persian art emerged only recently and at first was only concerned with painting and lacquer ware.

However, mass-produced objects such as ceramics and metalwork, which were used by a wide cross-section of society, bear witness to a clear decline

Shah Abbas and Khan Alam. By Riza-i Abbasi. ▶
17 Rajab 1042 AH/28 January 1633 AD
17.5 x 28.5cm. The National Library of Russia,
St Petersburg.
Inv. No. Dom 489, f. 74a.

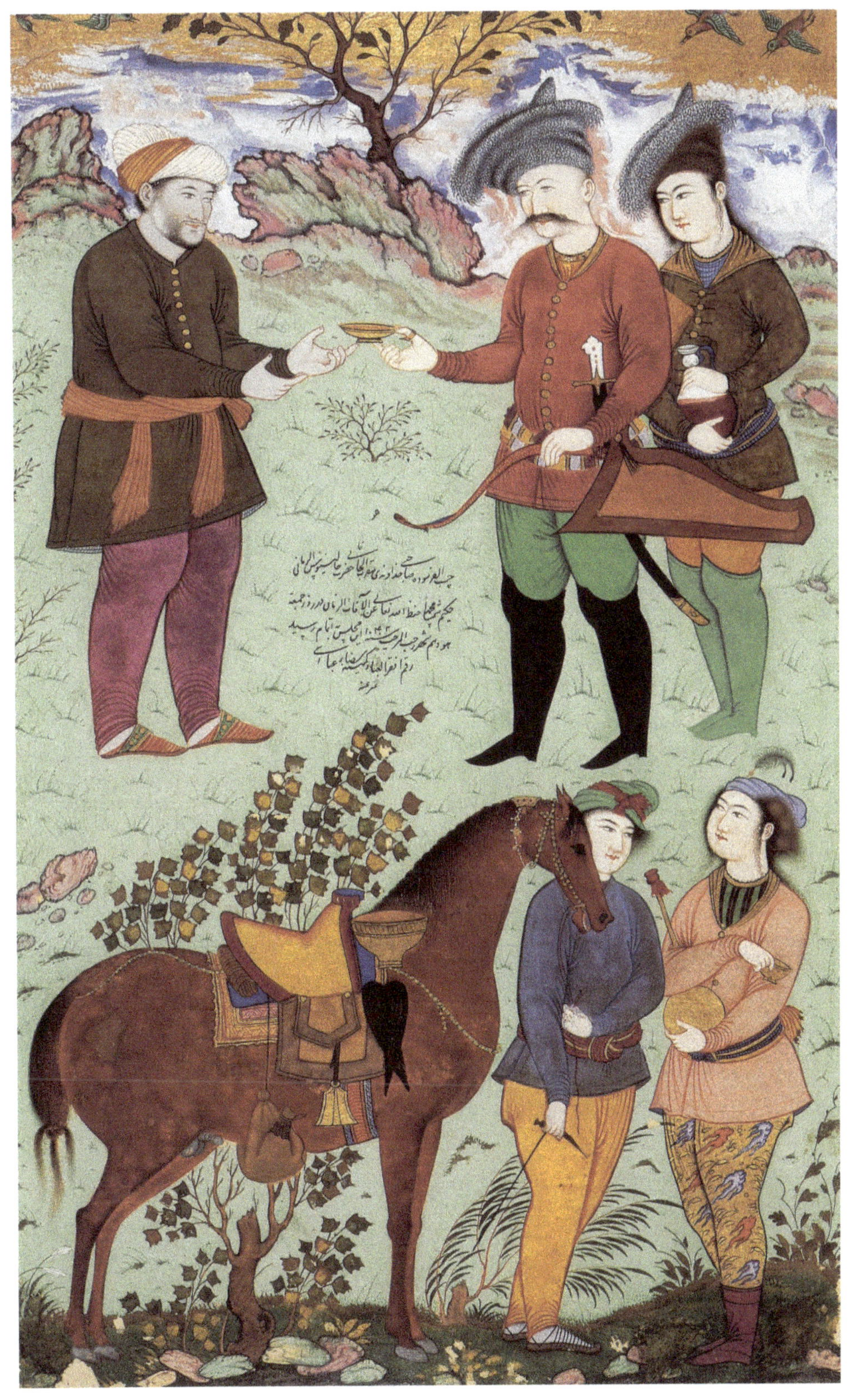

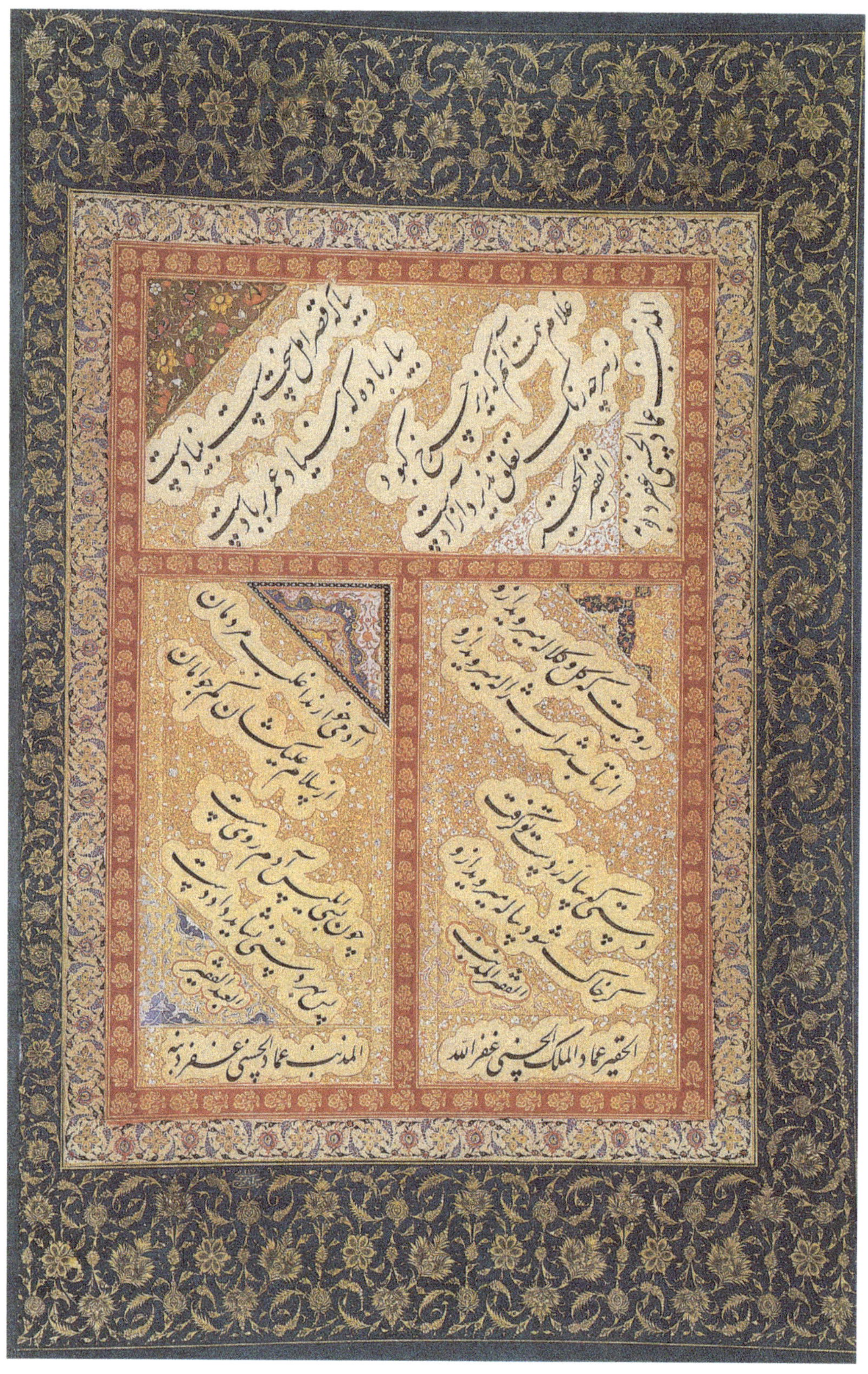

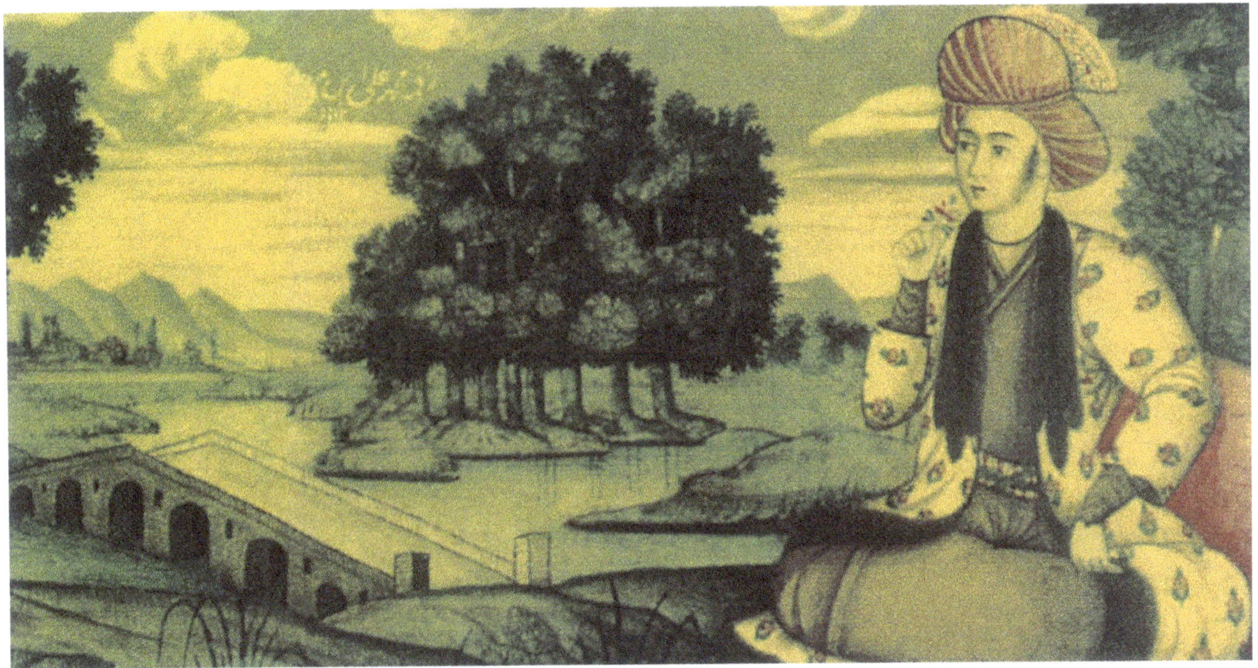

◀ Three samples of calligraphy. By Mir Imad.
No later than 1615
Indian ink on paper. Size of sheet: 45 x 29.5cm; size of samples: 19.4 x
9.4cm (upper), 17.5 x 9cm (left), 17.5 x9.2 cm (right).
Branch of the Institute of Oriental Studies of the Russian Academy of Sciences, St Petersburg (album E 14, sheet 95b).
Transferred 1921 from the Russian Museum, Petrograd.

▲ Box with hinged lid.
By Muhammad-Ali ibn
Muhammad-Zaman.
1112 AH/1700–01 AD
Papier-mâché, painted and lacquered. 26.9 x 6 x 4.8cm.
The Hermitage, St Petersburg.
Inv. No. VR-126. Transferred 1924 from the museum attached to the former Stieglitz School of Technical Design..

in technical skill. The crisis as a whole begins in the 1840s, when Persian art fell into a decline as a result of the factory goods from European countries which poured into Iran at that time. The rejection of old miniature painting techniques and the definite acceptance of European ones, date from the same period.

In conclusion, we wish to quote a statement by Nikolai Konradina's work *On the Meaning of History: In different lands, humanists have seen different aspects of the human personality as constituting its value. Their views have naturally been contingent upon their historical circumstances. Participants in the Chinese Renaissance saw the value of the personality chiefly in the human ability to attain self-perfection; the humanists of Iran and Central Asia saw it, mainly, in the fact that the highest moral qualities are accessible to man: spiritual nobility, magnanimity, friendship; the representatives of the Italian Renaissance regarded human beings as, above all, the bearers of reason, considering reason to be the highest manifestation of humanity's essence.*

LIST OF ILLUSTRATIONS

ART HISTORY COLLECTION

Abstract Art		Naive Art
Art Deco		Neoclassicism
Art Nouveau		Persian Art
Baroque		Post-Impressionism
Byzantine Art		Realism
Chinese Art		Renaissance
Cubism		Pre-Raphaelites
Dada		Rococo
Early Italian Art		Roman Art
Egypt Art		Romanesque Art
Expressionism		Romanticism
Gothic Art		Surrealism
Greek Art		Symbolism
Impressionism		The Fauves
Indian Art		The Viennese Secession